12/17

The **ACT**® for

testtakers

The **ACT**® for

testtakers

Moshe Ohayon

ISBN: 978-0-9887609-0-5

Published by:
Bad Test Takers
P.O. Box 8004
Louisville, KY 40257
www.BadTestTakers.com

ACT® is a registered trademark of ACT, Inc.

ACT, Inc. was not involved in the production of, and does not endorse, this product.

Table of Contents

Acknowledgements

First and foremost, I gratefully acknowledge the support of the entire Bad Test Takers team of ACT tutors, interns, consultants, and staff, including Alexa, Billy, Blake, Clare, Elisabeth, Haley, Holden, Jessica, Laura, Mason, Matthew, Sam, Sandra, Sarah H., Sarah S., and Sarah W.

I would also like to acknowledge Susan Duffy for her outstanding artwork, Robert Wright for his expert legal guidance, and Gretchen Sunderland for her words of moral support.

Next, I wish to thank all of the wonderful students I've had the privilege of tutoring over the years. I would especially like to acknowledge those who were with me in those early years and were patient enough to be my guinea pigs as the strategy was still evolving and being fine-tuned, including Aaron, Aida, Allison, Andreas, Anna, Barth, Brad, Breck, Connor, Cormel, Grady, Greg, Haggai, Haley, Harris, Jackson, Jesse, Jessi, Jon, Judy, Kaitlyn, Katharine, Katie, Keaton, Kenny, Kevin, Kiara, Lauren, Lev, Logan, Macy, Madison, Marc, Margaret, Michelle, Morgan, Nadav, Roderick, Ryan, Sadie, Sandra, Sara, Tiffany, Tipton, and Will.

Finally, I wish to acknowledge my family for continually inspiring me.

ACKNOWLEDGEMENTS

Matt, for effectively being my business manager, for believing in me even when I did not, and for giving me the confidence to see this through.

My parents, Fany and Israel, for their unconditional support and belief in my abilities.

And last, but certainly not least, my niece Sharon and nephew Avi, for effortlessly making me laugh, especially at the end of a long day.

Part 1
A New Approach
to the ACT

Introduction

If you're reading this, odds are that you're a bit nervous about an upcoming ACT exam. Odds are also good that you think of yourself as a bad test taker, and you're hoping that this guide will show you how to magically do well on the ACT. Well, we can't promise magic, but we *can* promise a successful strategy that will help you no matter where you are in your ACT journey.

IS THIS BOOK FOR YOU?

If you plan on taking the ACT, the short answer is yes, this book is for you. However, this book is really meant for the average test taker. If you have a score of 23 or lower in any one of the four sections of the test, this book is especially for you. But, even if you scored above a 23, this book will still give you some great insights into how to strategically prepare for the ACT.

HOW TO GET THE MOST OUT OF THIS BOOK

This book was inspired by our Crash Course videos, which are available at www.BadTestTakers.com. If you can, we highly recommend that you view those videos as well. But even if you don't get a chance to do so, we suggest you print out our free guide sheet, the *BTT Mental Map*, which is available on our website under *Resources*. The *BTT Mental Map* was specifically designed to guide you in taking notes on the critical parts of the strategy as you read this book or watch the videos. It is a great tool that will help cement the strategy in your mind.

Also, when you sit down to read this book, we want you to have two real ACT tests in front of you: ACT test form 0661C and ACT test form 1267C. Links to both of these test forms are also on the *Resources* page of our website. Ideally, we would like you to print them out and have them physically in your hands. But, if you don't have access to a printer, at least have them on the computer screen in front of you. We refer to those two tests throughout this book, and having them in front of you will make it much easier when we discuss them. Having physical copies in front of you is preferable because, when we talk about our attack strategy for the ACT, we want you to actually flip through the pages of these tests and verify that the numbers we are giving you are correct.

BAD testtakers TIP

We have also made some additional free tools available on our website, including links to more real ACT tests, success stories from our students, statistics about the ACT, and much more. Simply visit BadTestTakers.com and click on *Resources*.

We've included some illustrations throughout the book that we hope you'll find helpful, as well a few **TIP** boxes (like the one above) scattered along the way. At the end of the book, we've added a truly useful *Frequently Asked Questions* section, which includes our responses to some great questions our students have asked us over the years.

Before we move on, we want to urge you to read this book from cover to cover in order to get the full scope of our strategy. In fact, we recommend that you read this book multiple times, preferably every three weeks or so in order to keep the strategy fresh in your mind, and then again a week before the actual ACT. Not only understanding but really *internalizing* the complete strategy is key to using it effectively on test day.

WHY WE FOCUS ON STRATEGY IN THIS BOOK

This book is about strategy and not content. But when we tutor students, we work primarily on content. By content, we mean, for example, teaching how to successfully answer a question on the English section that tests the difference between *who* and *whom*, or the quickest way to solve a certain type of geometry problem on the Math section. Obviously, we think content is extremely important. So why aren't we teaching you content here?

Well, we realized early on that our students lacked an over-arching strategy for attacking the ACT. Most test takers, if they prepare at all, focus all their energy working on content and don't spend any time or effort developing a "big picture" approach to the ACT. As a result, these test takers think about the ACT in the same way as they've been programmed to think about a test in school, and that often turns them into bad test takers.

That's where we come in. Our goal with this book is really to reprogram you. We want you to look at the ACT in a particular way instead of the way that you have been approaching it until now. We want you to have a game plan for attacking this test in a logical, systematic way. We want to turn you into a good test taker. To do that, we need you to really understand this strategy first.

Is content still important? Definitely. So we don't want you to get the impression that strategy is all you need to do well on the ACT. But, since we think you need a practical, global approach to the ACT before you can tackle its content, we are saving discussions about content for our forthcoming books on each section.

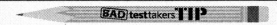

If you're interested in our methods for how to attack the ACT's content, our prep books on content-specific techniques for the four sections of the ACT are coming soon and will be a continuation of the approach you'll learn here. Look for the first, covering the English section, to be out soon!

To begin, let us tell you how we developed our expertise.

Chapter 1
Why You Should Listen to Us

It's important to know why we're a credible source for learning how to do well on the ACT. After all, you wouldn't want someone who never attended medical school (or who flunked out of medical school) to operate on you, right? Using that same logic, you should want people who actually know the ins and outs of the ACT to give you advice on how to excel on the ACT.

So who are we? We are a team of professional tutors who help students excel on the ACT. Some of us are still in college, while others have earned advanced degrees. But more importantly, we were once bad test takers ourselves; we weren't born with whatever genetic blessing it is that makes some people really do well on standardized tests with little to no effort. We didn't get 36s when we first took our ACTs in high school. In fact, we personally know the frustration that comes from doing OK or even well in school and feeling like your standardized test scores don't really reflect your ability.

But we came to understand that what works in school doesn't directly translate to success on the ACT, and that shouldn't be surprising since, while the two are similar, they also differ in significant ways. Think about this: ping pong and tennis are similar in some obvious ways, right? Both games use a ball, and players stand at opposing sides separated by a net in the middle. Even the paddle in ping pong has a similar shape to the racquet used in tennis. But someone who is great at ping pong wouldn't automatically be awesome at tennis, right? Of course not. In the same way, someone who is great at school isn't immediately awesome at the ACT, even though the sections on the ACT test the same types of subjects as those taught in school.

While we didn't have stellar results when we first took our ACTs, we got better at it. How? We have since studied this test like crazy and have become experts at it. We have literally spent thousands of hours studying how the ACT is scored, the types of questions the ACT asks, the patterns that the ACT uses, and everything else we could find out about the ACT.

We still take ACTs to test ourselves and to test the effectiveness of our strategies; we still wake up at 8 a.m. on the occasional weekend to go take the ACT at actual test centers so that we can put ourselves in your shoes. Honestly, we really dread doing it. It's not fun to go through that nearly 4-hour ordeal on a Saturday, especially when everyone stares at you because you're the oldest test taker in the room. But, we want to make sure our strategy works, so we keep taking it. We also want to make sure that we keep perspective on what it's like to take this test.

So, how do we score on the ACT? We regularly score in the 99th percentile, which means we get scores between 33 and 36. That may sound impressive, but notice that we don't get a 36 every time. Why? Because we're human, just like you. That's right! We make careless mistakes too, and we understand that almost all test takers make careless errors. The important difference is that we minimize them, and we teach our students how to do the same thing.

We decided to take our knowledge of the ACT and start a tutoring company to help other bad test takers. Over the years, we've tutored thousands of students. Many students come to us as sophomores with scores between 19 and 22, and we help them achieve scores between 25 and 31 by the end of their junior years. We've had many students come to us with scores in the mid-to-high 20s, and we've helped them achieve scores in the 30s. One student prepared for the ACT for over a year and raised her score by nine points! Another, who started with us as a sophomore with a score of 18, last took the test in June of her junior year and scored a 28; her highest individual score was a 32 in the English section, which is especially impressive considering English is her second language!

What if you're not a sophomore? Don't panic. Most of our students come to us in their late junior years or their senior years, and we are still successful in helping them boost their scores. In fact, we specialize in helping students with an average, or even below average, score who just want to do well enough to get into a certain college; this is the type of student we see the most.

We begin by working with our students through what we call a *cycle*, which is the time between ACT test dates, usually about two to four months. In the first cycle, we teach them our global strategy and begin working with them on how to practice. We then move on to content. After one or two cycles, these students tend to improve their scores by three to five points.

We regularly get students who have scores between 17 and 20 and work with them to improve to scores between 22 and 25 within just one or two cycles.

Students who stick with us for three to five cycles regularly score in the 30s.

But these results don't come overnight; our students make great gains only after a lot of hard work practicing with an effective strategy. But, even after reaching their target scores, they *almost always* say that they wish they had started with us earlier. They realize that the test is *learnable* and *beatable*, and they correctly recognize that starting early makes all the difference.

Here's an extraordinary case of what getting a head start on the ACT can do. One of our head tutors started working with a 7th grade student. That student is now a sophomore who scores a 30 or higher on every section of the ACT. Another extraordinary case: we had a student who started with us when he was in 9th grade. Today, he's a junior, and when he recently took the ACT, he scored a 33 on the English section, a 36 on the Math section, a 31 on the Reading section, and a 34 on the Science section. That's a composite score of 34. Most of these students' friends probably think they're natural-born test takers, but they simply started early, mastered our strategy, and practiced a lot.

One final word about us: many test prep companies prepare students by basically teaching school over again. We don't. We have found that re-teaching school is a waste of your time, because the ACT is not school. The ACT doesn't work in the same way that tests at school do.

We'll talk more about that in later in Chapter 3. Right now, let's talk about the most important and neglected component of any successful strategy for conquering the ACT.

Chapter 2
The Real Key to Success on the ACT

While we do have a unique strategy that will help you achieve a higher ACT score, it's not magic, and it's not a quick fix. Our strategy is useful whether you're taking the test in a month or in a year, but relying on strategy alone is not the best way to prepare for the ACT. The best way to prepare for the ACT is a word no one likes to hear: *practice.*

This is similar to the two things most people don't want to hear about from their doctor: diet and exercise. It's because most people want a magic formula, and they don't like the idea of putting in the work.

But you need to understand something: we can give you a revolutionary strategy, but to really boost your ACT score, there is no way to avoid doing practice. We could give you the most amazing car in the world, but without some form of fuel, the car wouldn't go anywhere. Similarly, we're about to teach you a powerfully effective approach for attacking the ACT, but it relies on practice to propel it. The more practice you have, the better the strategy works and the better you do on the ACT.

WHEN TO START

If you can, you should start practicing when you're a freshman or sophomore in high school. That gives you an entire year or more to gradually learn to implement the strategy and to do a great deal of practice without a great deal of pressure. If you can't start that early, start as early as you can. Ideally, you should be done with your ACT prep and take the ACT for the last time by the end of your junior year.

Why not take the ACT your senior year? It's fine, if it's an absolute must. Many of our students do, in fact, take the ACT in their senior years. But, that is far from ideal. Your senior year has the potential to be entirely too busy to prepare adequately for the ACT. You'll have your regular school classes, some of which may be really demanding, like AP or IB courses. Plus, there are college and scholarship applications to complete, extracurricular activities, college visits, etc. All of these things take up time and can be very stressful. So, you definitely don't want to be studying for and stressing out about the ACT on top of all that, if you can avoid it.

WHAT TO PRACTICE

The amount of time invested in practice matters, but equally important is the *type* of practice you do. The best form of practice is to do questions. We mean actual ACT questions, not questions from your Math or English book. While many test prep books can be useful in some circumstances, the questions in those books are not real ACT questions, and there is no guarantee that questions like those will appear on the ACT. We don't want you to spend valuable time and money answering questions that might not do you any good on the ACT.

Instead, spend that time answering questions from ACTs that were actually given in the past. While those *exact* questions are very unlikely to be on your exam, the ACT recycles *types* of questions over and over. For example, we've seen math questions on different ACT test forms where only the numbers were different. Getting used to those types of questions and learning how to do well on them is the best use of your practice time.

By the way, we DO NOT suggest that you use online prep even if the questions are real ACT questions. The ACT is a paper-based exam, and you should try to mimic testing conditions whenever possible. Even if you have real ACT questions, they need to be done on paper and *not* on the computer.

BAD testtakers TIP

On its website, the ACT offers several online practice options and even has an *ACT Question of the Day*. These can be great resources, so we encourage you to use them. But if you do, make sure that you print the questions out and work them out on paper.

NUMBER OF PRACTICE QUESTIONS

How many practice questions should you do? Ten certainly isn't enough. One hundred sounds like a good amount, until you discover that there are 215 questions on the ACT. One hundred questions is not even an entire practice test! We have found that our students start to do well on the ACT after about five practice tests, and those who do extremely well do more like 10 to 15 practice tests. That sounds like a lot of work, but that's why we recommend you start practicing your sophomore year. That way, it can be spread out comfortably and without as much pressure over a couple of years.

If you are a junior or a senior, you can still improve your score quite a bit, but you have to commit to doing all that practice in a shorter period of time. The more practice you do, the easier the questions become, the more repetitive and mundane the test becomes, and the better you do on the ACT when you take it for real.

Ideally, you would do as many practice questions as humanly possible, but if you can't do that, we definitely recommend doing at least five full practice tests. Be sure to push yourself, though. If you've done five practice tests, try for six or six and a half practice tests. Every question you do is worth it.

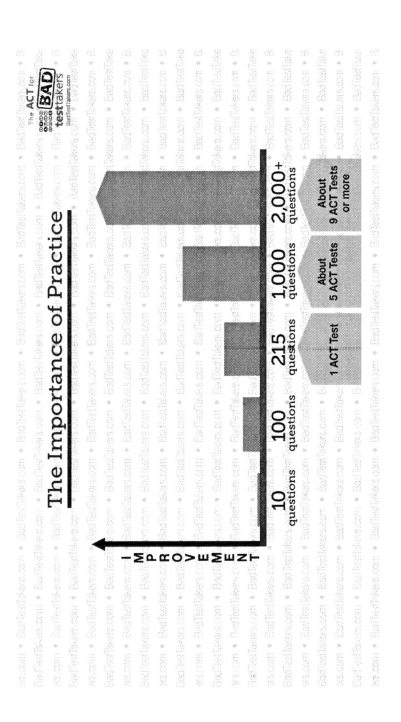

The Importance of Practice

IMPROVEMENT

10 questions | 100 questions | 215 questions | 1,000 questions | 2,000+ questions

1 ACT Test | About 5 ACT Tests | About 9 ACT Tests or more

And now, you might be wondering: *where do I get these ACT questions I'm supposed to be using to practice?* The ACT's website offers a practice test (currently it's ACT test form 1267C) for free that you can print out and complete. Additionally, the ACT publishes a book called The Real ACT Prep Guide, which includes five retired ACT tests. We really like this book not just because it has actual ACT questions, but also because it contains an explanation for each question instead of giving you only the correct answer and expecting you to puzzle it out yourself. Some of the explanations in the book are better than others, but having some kind of explanation is still (usually) better than none at all.

BAD testtakers TIP

You can find a link to the newest edition of *The Real ACT Prep Guide* as well as to other previously-released ACT practice tests on our website, BadTestTakers.com, under *Resources*.

That's six tests, which is enough for you to see a significant improvement in your score. That also meets our strongly recommended minimum of five practice tests.

But what if you want to do more practice? The ACT has also released other practice tests over the years. On our website under *Resources*, you can find links to these retired tests that we found by simply searching the internet.

Finally, if you need additional tests, we highly recommend using the ACT's Test Information Release (TIR) service, which we talk a lot more about in Chapter 10.

WHERE TO PRACTICE

Some test takers like to practice in complete silence, but this can backfire. After all, the testing center is not going to be completely silent. There's always that one person with a cough, and the person behind you may be nervously munching on his or her pencil.

We suggest studying somewhere like a library where there is some background noise. But if you're easily distracted, we actually recommend studying somewhere like a coffee shop that has more noise than you are likely to have on test day but isn't excessively noisy. It will be tough at first, but it will help you hone your ability to block out background noise. With practice, you'd be surprised how quickly you can adapt to tuning out distractions.

HOW TO PRACTICE

- Try to mimic real test conditions as closely as possible.

- Start by taking untimed sections until you gain familiarity with the test and how to implement our strategy.

- Once you've mastered the strategy and have done some untimed practice, time yourself on each section of the test just as if it were an actual ACT.

- Use a real ACT answer sheet when doing timed practice sections. There are several copies of the ACT answer sheet available in The Real ACT Prep Guide, and one on page 74 of ACT test form 1267C.

BAD testtakers TIP

When you're taking a practice test, instead of bubbling in your answer after every question, simply circle the answers in your test booklet. Then, just before you turn a page in your test booklet, transfer your answers to the bubble sheet in bulk. This will save you some of the time typically lost to bubbling. It also allows you to keep your bubble sheet under your test booklet and only bring it out just before you flip a page to transfer your answers. Added benefits: your concentration isn't broken as often, and you save time by not shuffling papers as much. To become comfortable with this technique, be sure to implement it in your practice sessions.

- Use a regular pencil (not mechanical) to mark your answers.

- Use the exact same calculator that you will be using on the day of the ACT.

- At least on the four Saturdays leading up to the ACT, force yourself to wake up early and take a practice test at 8 a.m. That will help condition you to take the actual test, which is offered at 8 a.m. on a Saturday.

Ideally, when doing practice questions, we'd like you to go back and review all of your answers. Yes, we mean *all* the answers, not just the ones you missed. Students usually don't have issues going over their wrong answers, but students are often reluctant to review their correct answers. However, students who do it have greater gains. Why should correct answers not be neglected? It's possible that you guessed on some of the questions you answered correctly or that you reached a correct answer by incorrect means. You need to know why the correct answer is correct and why the other answers are wrong. If you cannot explain to a friend why the correct answer is correct and why the other answer choices are wrong, spend more time studying that question until you figure it out rather than just moving on. You need to make sure you genuinely know how to arrive at the correct answer so that you can apply a repeatable method on the day of the ACT.

[BAD] test takers TIP

We teach our students to develop a habit of marking answer choices that they found *tempting* but did not choose. For example, if you correctly chose D but also thought B was a good answer choice while you were taking the test, it's helpful if you had somehow marked B so that you could go back and review it to figure out why it was not the right answer choice.

We've seen our students use a question mark, a star, or a semicircle to mark tempting answer choices. Feel free to choose one of these or make up a different one that works for you, but be sure to incorporate this habit into your practice.

Finally, the Test Information Release (TIR) service we mentioned earlier is a great resource. We have our students take advantage of this little-known gem to really maximize the effect of practice. Again, we'll talk more about what makes the TIR a useful tool in Chapter 10.

(BAD) testtakers TIP

If you have a very limited amount of time before the ACT, we think it's more important that you do a large number of practice questions than spend time going back to review every single one of your answers after a practice test. In such a case, we suggest just reviewing (1) the questions you got wrong, (2) the questions you guessed on, and (3) the questions where you marked a choice as *tempting*. Going back to make sure you really study and understand these three groups of questions will be the most efficient use of your limited practice time.

That's enough about practice for the moment. Later, in our FAQs section, we'll share our best tips for *how to get the most out of your practice*.

What Makes For Effective Practice?

1. Practice with real (retired) ACT tests.
- Begin by doing untimed practice.

2. Practice under "real" test conditions.
- Time yourself.
- Use an ACT answer sheet.
- Use a nonmechanical pencil.
- Use the actual calculator you will use on test day.

Ⓐ Ⓑ Ⓒ Ⓓ

Ⓐ Ⓑ ● Ⓓ

Ⓕ Ⓖ Ⓗ ●

✗

3. Review all answers.
- Review incorrect responses.
  Make sure you understand why your answer is wrong.
- Review correct responses.
  Make sure you understand why your answer is correct and why the other choices are wrong.

4. Register and take the ACT multiple times.
- Register for TIR administrations whenever possible.
- Always order the TIR.

Chapter 3
What You Need to Know About How the ACT Is Scored

Let's lay the groundwork for our strategy by telling you the important aspects of how the test is scored.

While most students know that the highest score possible on the ACT is 36, not everyone knows that the lowest score is 1. Currently, the ACT is offered six times a year nationally:

- February

- April

- June

- September

- October

- December

At each administration (or offering) of the test, about a quarter of a million test takers take the ACT. That's about 1.5 million test takers each year! We estimate that the annual number of test takers will surpass 2 million before the end of the decade.

You might expect that with so many test takers, we would see great variability in how many people get each of the available 36 scores. However, that isn't what we see at all. The scores on the ACT from administration to administration and year to year are remarkably similar. Why? Simple: the test is designed to work that way.

The ACT writes and scales the test in such a way that from administration to administration, there is roughly the same percentage of each score. The ACT can't possibly ensure that every test is exactly the same level of difficulty as every test before it. It makes sense, then, that they would scale tests that were really hard so that a person who was unlucky enough to sign up for that administration doesn't get lower scores than someone with "the same ability" who was lucky enough to sign up for an easy administration at a different time.

We'll explain by giving you a hypothetical example. Let's say, on an October ACT, Alice got 29 out of the 40 questions correct on the Reading section and got a score of 28 on that Section. Bruce also got 29 questions correct on the Reading section when he took the ACT, but he took it in December and got a score of 23 on that section. That seems unfair, right? After all, they got the same number of questions correct.

Think about what happened, though. Alice's test was much harder, so she probably had to work harder and spend more time on each question in order to get those 29 questions right. Bruce's test was easier, and he probably didn't have to work

34

as hard or spend as much time to get his 29 correct answers. Bruce shouldn't get the same score as Alice when his exam was easier; that would be an unfair advantage.

The ACT uses a "curve" to make sure that doesn't happen. So, Bruce gets a lower score than Alice for answering 29 out of 40 questions correct, because Alice answered the same number of questions on a harder test. But what's interesting is that each time the ACT is given, the distribution of scores is almost exactly the same regardless of how difficult the exam is.

Let's talk about the range of possible scores. We all know that very few test takers get a 36, and that makes sense because it's not easy to do. But even fewer get a 1, mostly because no one *wants* to get a 1, but also because it's not easy to get a 1 either, assuming you actually bubble in answers on the test. Why? Because most of the questions on the ACT (i.e., those on the English, Reading, and Science sections) have four answer choices and only one correct answer. On those questions, if you're just guessing, you have a 75% chance of getting the question wrong and a 25% chance of getting the question right.

On the Math section, your odds are worse because there are five answer choices, so you have an 80% chance of getting the question wrong and a 20% chance of getting the question right when you guess. That means that, even if a test taker went through the entire exam and answered every question randomly, he or she would get about one-fourth of the answers right. To get a 1, someone would have to deliberately pick the wrong answer for every question, which is not an easy task. (Obviously, if someone really wanted to get a 1, it would be easier to just turn in a blank bubble sheet.)

But that brings up an interesting observation. A test taker who just guesses on every question will not get a 1; in fact, he or she is most likely to score about a 12. Even if that person has a bad guessing day, he or she would likely get no lower than a 9. Interestingly, the number of test takers who score a 9 is not just small; it's roughly the same as the number of test takers who score a 36. Test takers who score below a 9 are extremely few in number. These are situations in which someone started the test but probably left it mostly incomplete for one reason or another. That means that the highest score is a 36, and the lowest score, for our purposes, is something like a 9.

If we think about all of the possible ACT scores being on a number line, we can remove all the scores lower than 9. We talked about how statistically improbable it is to get a score below 9 and how few people do, so we're going to take them out of the picture just to make explaining the strategy a bit easier.

But what about the scores in the middle? The national average score on the ACT is a 21. Not surprisingly, the most common score on the ACT is almost always the same as the average score or very close to it. For example, the ACT's data for 2009 show that the most common score was a 20, which is very close to the average.

The ACT for **BAD** testtakers
BadTestTakers.com

9   16   19   20   21   22   25   30   36

*This is a simplification intended to provide a general strategic framework for viewing the ACT and not a rigorous statistical analysis. Simplification is based on data drawn from ACT Profile Report – National. *Graduating Class 2009.* Page 10. See <http://www.act.org/newsroom/data/2009/pdf/National2009.pdf>.

Why does the most common score tend to be the same as the average score (or very near it)? Remember that the average equals the sum of all of the scores divided by the number of test takers. The most common score doesn't have to be the average, but it makes sense that it ought to be close to the average, especially if we have a large number of test takers like the quarter of a million or so who take the test at each national administration of the ACT.

To make this easier to understand, let's take an example. Say we have ten ACT test takers. They get scores of 13, 15, 18, 20, 20, 21, 22, 24, 25, and 28. Taking a look at the list of scores, 20 is the most common score. But, if you average those numbers, you get 20.6, which the ACT rounds up to 21. Now, obviously this happens on a much greater scale and with many more types of scores on a real test administration, but we wanted to give this example to illustrate what we're talking about.

What you might find shocking is that about 50% of the people who take the ACT get a score between 17 and 23. Let us repeat that. *About half* of the people who take the ACT score somewhere between 17 and 23. That's a lot of people for only seven scores out of a possible set of 36!

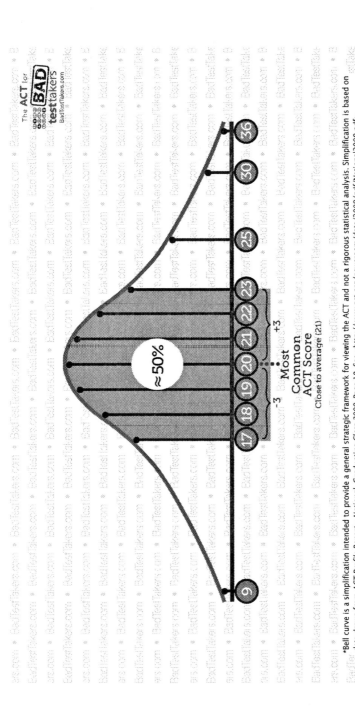

*Bell curve is a simplification intended to provide a general strategic framework for viewing the ACT and not a rigorous statistical analysis. Simplification is based on data drawn from *ACT Profile Report - National. Graduating Class 2009.* Page 10. See <http://www.act.org/newsroom/data/2009/pdf/National2009.pdf>.

Roughly 20% of test takers get scores between 1 and 16. That means it takes sixteen scores to account for the bottom 20%, but only seven scores to account for the middle 50%. The remaining 30% or so of test takers get a score from 24 to 36.

This distribution of scores may seem bizarre, but it's statistically expected. The distribution begins to resemble a bell curve. What all this is meant to illustrate is that your score on the ACT is relative, which we will discuss more a little later on. For now, just keep in mind that earning a score of 24, for example, means doing better than about 70% of the other test takers.

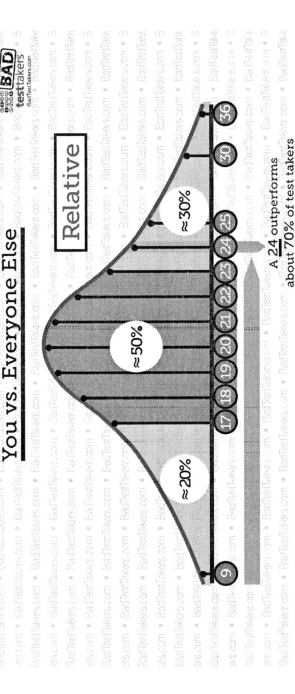

The ACT for **BAD** testtakers
BadTestTakers.com

You vs. Everyone Else

Relative

≈20%   ≈50%   ≈30%

9   17 18 19 20 21 22 23 24 25   30   36

A **24** outperforms about 70% of test takers

*Bell curve is a simplification intended to provide a general strategic framework for viewing the ACT and not a rigorous statistical analysis. Simplification is based on data drawn from *ACT Profile Report - National. Graduating Class 2009*. Page 10. See <http://www.act.org/newsroom/data/2009/pdf/National2009.pdf>.

Before we move on, we need to make sure you know a couple of things about ACT scoring. Points are not taken off for wrong answers, so you might as well guess if you don't know the answer. That means that you should fill in an answer for every question on the ACT, even if it's just a guess.

Also, remember that your score on the ACT is influenced by how other test takers do on the test. Some test takers think that their scores are based only on their own performance, but that's simply not true. Because the percentages on the bell curve determine the scores, if you did well on one administration of the ACT but other test takers tended to do *really* well on that same ACT, you will get a lower score. If you did well but other test takers tended to do *really* poorly, you will get a higher score. Scoring on the ACT is relative.

Speaking of relative scoring, students tend to bring a lot of ideas from the classroom into ACT prep that are not only unhelpful but actually counterproductive. We'll mention one idea in the next chapter and talk about it more fully in the following chapter on the English section. But first, let's talk about a scoring mindset from school that doesn't serve you well on the ACT.

Remember Bruce from our earlier example? He got 29 out of 40 questions correct on the Reading section of a given ACT and got a score of 23 on that section. A 23 is a pretty decent score and certainly not one to be ashamed of. However, if we were in school, getting 29 questions right out of 40 would only be 72.5%, which doesn't sound quite as good as a 23. Or, consider this: a score of 23 out of 36 only comes out to be about 64%, which is not a test score you would proudly put on your fridge. A 23 definitely sounds better!

The point of these examples is to show that *you*, as well as the makers of the ACT, judge an ACT score in a relative way. You don't consider the percent of questions you answered correctly or the percentage your score represents out of the highest possible score; it's just how you do compared to everyone else.

Chapter 4
Average Joe and Joan

We call the 50% or so of test takers who get a score between 17 and 23 *Average Joes and Average Joans, or just AJs* for short. Many test takers get AJ scores on the ACT not only because they lack knowledge about what's being tested, but also because they don't use an effective strategy.

The ACT operates based on the assumption that many more people will get a score near the average rather than far from it. But that's also the way the test is designed: to have a large number of AJs in the middle of the bell curve but few test takers near the extremes of the curve.

Most of our students start out as AJs. So, if right now you're thinking *I'm an AJ,* that's OK! It's now our job to show you how not to be. The goal of this book is to give you a strategy that will propel you out of the AJ zone and into the 30% zone. But to do that, we need to understand what the AJ does on the ACT.

We divide ACT test takers into three basic groups: those who score below a 17 (the 20% zone), AJs (the 50% zone), and those who score above a 23 (the 30% zone). It's impossible to know exactly what someone will do on a test, but we can generalize here to help you understand how most test takers approach this test.

Let's start with the people who get scores below 17. Those test takers don't answer a lot of questions correctly, probably don't finish the test, and may not even guess on questions they don't get to.

Not surprisingly, the people who get high scores on the ACT do exactly the opposite. They finish all (or almost all) of the exam and make sure to guess on any question they don't get to. More importantly, the overall quality of their responses is great; in other words, they get very few questions wrong.

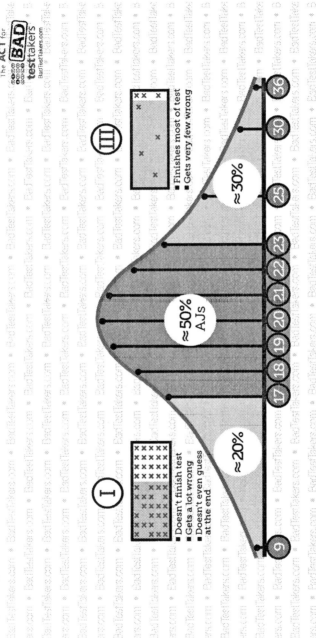

I

- Doesn't finish test
- Gets a lot wrong
- Doesn't even guess at the end

≈20%

≈50% AJs

≈30%

III

- Finishes most of test
- Gets very few wrong

*Bell curve is a simplification intended to provide a general strategic framework for viewing the ACT and not a rigorous statistical analysis. Simplification is based on data drawn from *ACT Profile Report - National. Graduating Class 2009.* Page 10. See <http://www.act.org/newsroom/data/2009/pdf/National2009.pdf>.

The ACT for **BAD** testtakers
BadTestTakers.com

But what about those in the middle of the curve? Those are the AJs. We think that AJs could largely be broken down into two hypothetical subgroups: (1) those who do a small part of the test very well but run out of time and end up guessing on more than half of it and (2) those who finish the entire test or close to it but move too quickly, making a lot of careless errors and guessing a lot.

Practically speaking, though, we don't see many students who fall into the first subgroup. Our experience shows that almost all AJs fall into the second subgroup because students believe that it is critically important to do whatever it takes to finish the test. In school, that may be true. But keep in mind that this is the ACT. We mentioned in the previous chapter that students tend to bring ideas from school into the ACT and that doing so can be counterproductive. This is another example of that.

As we go through our strategy for the English section of the ACT in Chapter 5, you will see how the test-taking mindset needed for the ACT is radically different than the one you picked up in school.

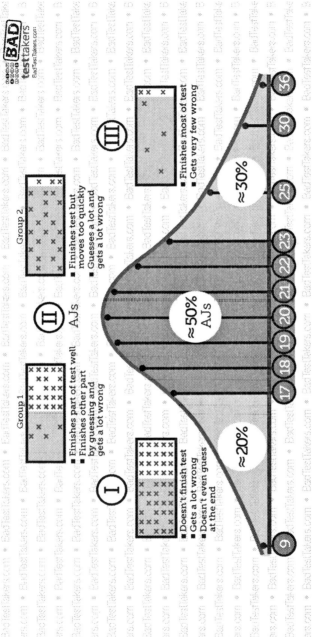

The ACT for
BAD testtakers
BadTestTakers.com

Group 1

(II) AJs

Group 2

(I)

(III)

≈50% AJs

≈20%

≈30%

9 17 18 19 20 21 22 23 25 30 36

Group 1
- Finishes part of test well
- Finishes other part by guessing and gets a lot wrong

Group 2
- Finishes test but moves too quickly
- Guesses a lot and gets a lot wrong

(I)
- Doesn't finish test
- Gets a lot wrong
- Doesn't even guess at the end

(III)
- Finishes most of test
- Gets very few wrong

*Bell curve is a simplification intended to provide a general strategic framework for viewing the ACT and not a rigorous statistical analysis. Simplification is based on data drawn from ACT Profile Report - National. Graduating Class 2009. Page 10. See <http://www.act.org/newsroom/data/2009/pdf/National2009.pdf>.

So, what do most AJs do? They focus too much on quantity at the expense of quality. They rush through most, if not all, of the ACT and don't spend enough time worrying about the quality of the work they do. When we say quality, we really mean how many questions a test taker gets right. There are no prizes for finishing the ACT. You don't get a score of 30 just for bubbling in an answer for every question on the answer sheet; you get a 30 for bubbling in a high number of *correct* answers on the answer sheet.

FORMAT

As we move closer to the core of our strategy, it is critical to introduce the format of each section of the ACT. Most test takers don't study the format of the test and miss out on several benefits. The primary benefit is that knowing the format gives us a mental map of the exam. That mental map helps us to pace ourselves during the test. Also, knowing the number of questions and passages in each section makes the test seem smaller and less like an endless exam, so having a mental map has the added benefit of helping to lower our anxiety about the test. After all, if you go into the exam having a good idea of what to expect, you'll probably be a little less anxious about it.

Most students don't invest time into learning the format because they don't believe it will translate into much of a score increase. To be perfectly honest, we agree. After all, knowing the format alone isn't likely going to boost someone's score from a 22 to a 28.

Most of our students think that knowing the ACT's format, even if it gives you all of the benefits we mentioned above, might make a difference of one or two points. An increase of one or two points may be possible for some test takers. But, based on our experience, we think that merely knowing the format of the test makes even less of a difference than that; we think it will more realistically translate into maybe a ½-point gain.

But, we think that ½ point shouldn't be underestimated. Why? Because your ACT composite score is the average of the scores you get on each of the four sections. It is the sum of four whole numbers divided by four, so you will always end up with a composite score ending in .0, .25, .5, or .75.

For example, after averaging the sections, someone could not only end up with a score of 22 or 23 but a score of 22.25, 22.5, or 22.75. The ACT will then round the score using the conventional method of rounding, so anyone who received a score of 22 or 22.25 would get a score of 22, and anyone who received a score of 22.5 or 22.75 would get rounded up to a score of 23.

We wondered why most test takers don't take 15 minutes to learn the format of the exam and commit it to memory. We believe it must be because they think it won't translate into any real increase in score. That might be what you're thinking. But even if it results in just a ½-point boost, we think you shouldn't rush to dismiss that. Now, if you earn a 22.5, getting an extra ½ point will give you a 23, which is what you would have gotten anyway. But, what if you get a 22 or 22.25? The extra ½ point would kick up your score to a 23. Who wouldn't rather get a 23 than a 22, or a 30 instead of a 29? We would argue that for just 15 minutes of prep to learn the format of the ACT, it's well worth it.

But we're guessing that you didn't pick up this book for ½-point increase, and we get that. We're going to show you how knowing the format of the ACT can result in a much greater score increase. But only those students who know the format of the ACT and know it well have access to such a strategy.

Chapter 5
English

First, remember that format is really important to our strategy, so let's begin there. We need to know how many questions there are, how they are divided up, and how much time we have to finish the section. Hopefully, you have in front of you the two real ACT tests that we mentioned previously so that you can check what we're telling you about the format and see it for yourself. We will be referring primarily to ACT test form 0661C, so it's important to have it handy so that you can follow along.

> ### [BAD]testtakers TIP
>
> If you haven't done so already, now is the time to print out (or pull up on your computer screen) two real ACT tests: form 0661C and form 1267C. Links to both are available on our website, BadTestTakers.com, under *Resources*.

In ACT test form 0661C, the English section begins on page 14. Take a minute to flip through the pages of the English section to get an idea of how it's structured. You'll notice that there are 75 questions and that you're given 45 minutes to answer them.

1. English

2. Math

3. Reading

4. Science

75
Questions

45
Minutes

54

When we ask if that's fair, most of our students immediately tell us that it is *so* unfair. Why? We think it's because most students start from the idea that a minute per question is fair, and this section allows less than a minute per question on average.

If you think about it, though, you will realize that a minute per question as a standard of fairness is arbitrary. If we gave you a test of ten questions in Swedish* and allowed you ten minutes to complete it, that would be horribly unfair. On the other hand, if we gave you a 26-minute test that asks you to name the letters of the English alphabet, you would have a ridiculous amount of extra time.

In our opinion, the English section turns out to be the most fair section on the ACT in terms of time because the average question requires about 30 seconds or less to answer.

The other thing you need to know about the format of the English section is that the 75 questions are divided into five passages of 15 questions each.

WHAT THE AJ DOES

The AJ gets about seven to ten correct out of the 15 questions in each passage. That surprised us at first, because we thought the average high school student would get a few more questions than that correct. But, other than lack of content knowledge, there are a number of factors that affect test takers. These collateral factors likely contribute towards bringing the AJ's performance down to only about seven to ten questions per passage.

---

*.   We're, of course, assuming that your knowledge of Swedish is non-existent (i.e., comparable to that of Peter Van Houten).

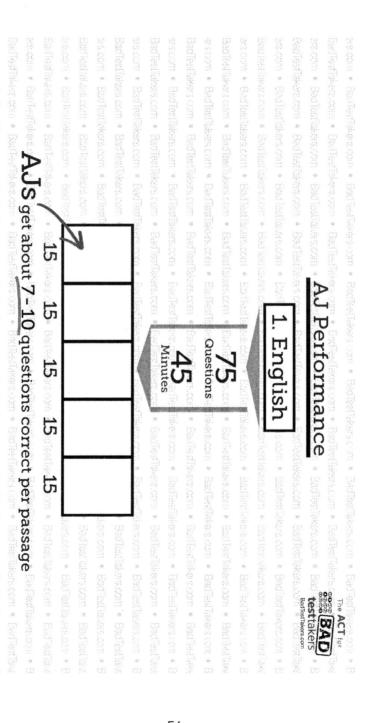

AJ Performance

1. English

75 Questions
45 Minutes

15   15   15   15   15

AJs get about 7-10 questions correct per passage

COLLATERAL FACTORS AFFECTING SCORES

First, AJs are very aware of the time pressure imposed by the ACT and rush through the test. They feel as though they absolutely must get through every single question on the test, even though they might miss easy questions because they're rushing. This is a mindset from school that doesn't carry over well into the ACT.

In school, if you don't finish one-fifth of a test, you'll probably get a grade that isn't very good. However, the ACT is relative, so if you finish the test but miss a bunch of questions because you're rushing, that's counterproductive. Remember, the ACT isn't going to give you extra points for finishing the test; they only score you on how many questions you get right.

Second, AJs often feel a lack of confidence in their ability to do well on the test. AJs may feel this way even though they do well in school and know their stuff. However, as we've talked about, the ACT does not work in the same way that a test given in school does.

In the previous chapter, we emphasized the importance of learning the format of the ACT and developing a mental map of its layout. Having such a mental map of the structure of the entire test can help to reduce your anxiety about it. But AJs often don't pay much attention to the format of the exam, figure out pacing, or come into the exam with a strategy. AJs also don't practice much or in an effective way, and so they don't get really comfortable with the ACT. As a result, they lack some confidence that they might otherwise have, and that brings their scores down.

Third, there are always distractions in the ACT. We mentioned the pencil-munching dude back in Chapter 2. One of our tutors took an exam once where the guy seated behind him sounded like he was actually dining on his pencil. Even if there's not a pencil-muncher in the room, it seems like someone is always sick and coughing up a lung on test day. And, even if a test taker gets lucky and doesn't have those distractions, there will always be rustling paper, scratching pencils, shifting chairs, and mournful sighs. These distractions could also be weighing down the AJs' scores.

Fourth, like everyone taking the ACT, AJs are bound to have anxiety. This test is a big deal for most test takers, and AJs are going to feel that anxiety just as much or more than test takers who do really well. We talked about some ways to help reduce anxiety over the exam (e.g., practicing, developing a mental map, and implementing a proven strategy), and it may be that AJs just don't do much to reduce their anxiety about the test.

Fifth is conditioning. Athletes condition themselves for competitions. The ACT is also a competition, much like a marathon. But most test takers don't build up their stamina for this test. In Chapter 2, we mentioned that the ACT is given at 8 a.m. on a Saturday. Most high school students are not accustomed to getting up at 8 a.m. on a Saturday to take what amounts to about a 4-hour test. That lack of conditioning could also hurt their scores a bit.

From all or a combination of these things, in addition to lack of content knowledge, the AJ often ends up with seven to ten correct answers per passage.

Collateral Factors
Affecting Score

- Pressure due to time
- Rushing
- Lack of confidence
- Distractions
- Unfamiliarity with test
- Anxiety
- No conditioning

The rushing and other factors that affect AJs all put together (but mostly the rushing) really make a difference. Let's consider a hypothetical AJ case. Say we have an AJ who gets seven questions right in the first passage, eight questions in the second passage, eight questions in the third passage, nine in the fourth passage, and eight in the last passage. That's a total of 40 questions correct out of 75 on the English section.

In school, that would earn you a 53%, but remember that we don't care. This is the ACT! Take a look at page 63 of ACT test form 0661C. The raw score conversion table on this page shows you what getting 40 questions right out of 75 questions on the English section of this test would translate to: an 18, which is what we'd call an AJ score.

Hypothetical Example of AJ Score

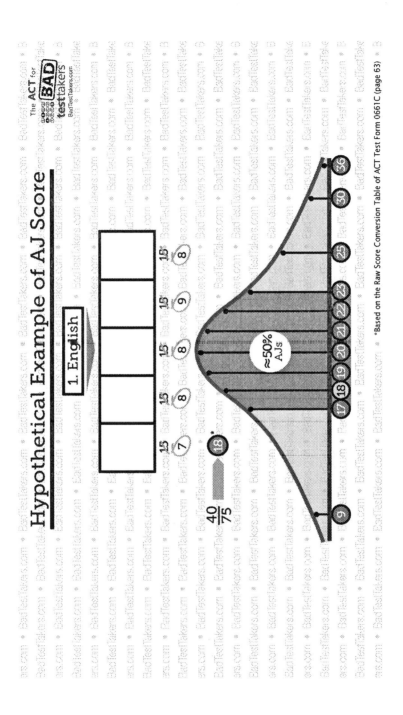

1. English

≈50% AJs

$\frac{40}{75}$ 18*

*Based on the Raw Score Conversion Table of ACT Test Form 0661C (page 63)

The ACT for **BAD testtakers**
BadTestTakers.com

61

THE STRATEGY

With most test takers, there is too much focus on quantity over quality. Test takers worry about quantity because of the time constraints, which results in not spending enough time on each question to get the correct answer. So, we teach our students a radically different approach. On the English section, we tell them to skip the last passage of 15 questions.

If that sounds crazy to you, that's OK. We know it sounds nuts. The scowl on your face is one we've seen many times before. Just hear us out. We just need to talk you past your AJ programming, and we promise it will make sense.

If you skip the last passage, that means you now have 45 minutes for only 60 questions instead of 75. That is a lot more time per question that test takers can use to make sure their response quality is excellent. In other words, it frees up time to allow them to do much better on those 60 questions than they would have done if they had followed the AJ tendency of rushing to finish the section at all costs.

But here's the catch: practice is required. You have to do enough practice problems to actually use that extra time effectively in order to do well on those first 60 questions. So, how well do you actually have to do on those 60 questions in order to get out of the AJ score range? Instead of getting only seven to ten questions correct, we expect our students to get 14 out of 15 correct on each of the first 4 passages.

Now, if you're paying attention, you should be freaking out. We just demanded that you get 14 out of 15 questions right on each passage of the English section. That's crazy, right?

There are two logical objections you should make at this point. One is: *I don't have the knowledge I need to get 14 out of 15 questions right.* This is a smart objection, but we've already given you our answer to it: practice. You acquire the knowledge you need to get 14 out of 15 correct on each of the English passages by doing a ton of practice. This may sound tough to achieve, but we've managed to reach this goal time and again with countless students of various ages and skill levels. Why is it possible? Because the ACT tests the same things over and over, and doing effective practice accumulates the knowledge you need to get 14 out of 15 answers correct.

The second objection: *I don't have enough time to get 14 out of 15 questions right.* This may ordinarily be true, but we already took care of that and gave you more time. How? We told you not to do that last passage. Remember, you still have 45 minutes but now you only need to do 60 questions, which means you have more time to spend on each question in the first four passages.

So let's say you follow the strategy and get 14 out of 15 on the first four passages. If you do that, you may only have 30 seconds left when you get to the last passage, which clearly isn't enough time to do another passage. But that doesn't matter because you have already gotten 56 questions right out of 75. Take a look again at page 63 of ACT test form 0661C. Getting 56 questions correct would have given you a score of 24 on that test.

The ACT for
BAD
testtakers

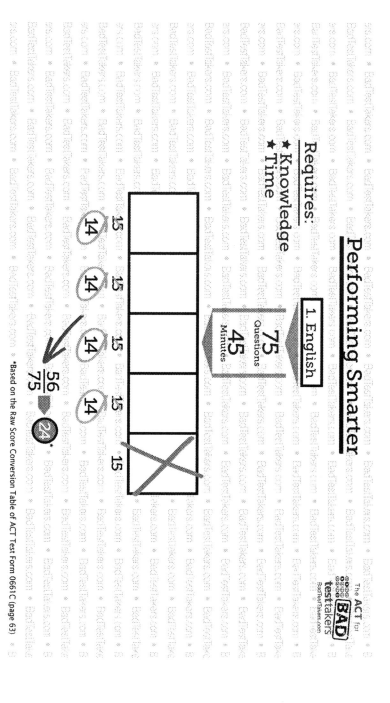

Performing Smarter

Requires:
- ★ Knowledge
- ★ Time

1. English

75 Questions

45 Minutes

15 | 15 | 15 | 15 | 15

(14) (14) (14) (14)

$\frac{56}{75}$ → 24*

*Based on the Raw Score Conversion Table of ACT Test Form 0661C (page 63)

That's not too bad, and it's a little better than an AJ does. But what about that last passage? Well, if all you have is 30 seconds left, that's not enough time to do it, but it is enough time to guess. That's right. Just guess on every single answer in the last passage.

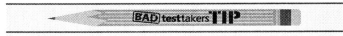

Check out the FAQs at the end of the book to see which letter we think you should guess.

Remember that your chance of guessing right is 25% because, in each question, there are four answer choices but only one correct answer. That means you are likely to guess correctly on a fourth of those last 15 questions, so you should expect to get about four questions right.

That's four more questions than we had before, which brings our total up to 60 questions correct out of 75. According to page 63 of ACT test form 0661C, 60 questions correct out of 75 on the English section would have earned the test taker a score of 26.

So, let's recap. An AJ using an AJ strategy might get 40 questions right and get a score of 18. Someone who did the necessary amount of practice, acquired enough knowledge, and followed our strategy would get 60 questions right and get a score of 26. That is a huge difference, and that's exactly what we teach our students to do.

Requires:
★ Knowledge
★ Time

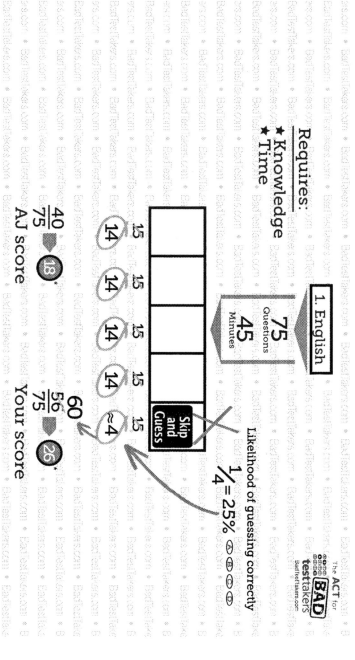

1. English
75 Questions
45 Minutes

15 15 15 15 15

14 14 14 14 ≈4

Skip and Guess

Likelihood of guessing correctly

$\frac{1}{4}$ = 25%

$\frac{40}{75}$ ➡ 18*

AJ score

$\frac{56}{75}$ ➡ 26*

60

Your score

*Based on the Raw Score Conversion Table of ACT Test Form 0661C (page 63)

66

Now, before you get too excited, remember that this strategy is *not* based on magic but on logic. We've taught *hundreds* of students to implement this strategy successfully. But, they *all* had to do the work; they were all committed to doing the necessary practice.

We just showed that it is better to focus on quality than quantity, but remember that you can take this too far. For example, you can't decide to do only one passage really well, get all 15 questions, and guess on the remaining 60. Quality is important, but it's not the whole story. There is a balance between quality and quantity for achieving any desirable score. In our experience, however, the majority of students focus too much on quantity and not enough on quality. So, our strategy is designed to correct that tendency.

By the way, when you get a much better score on the English section and tell your AJ friends about the new strategy you're using and how you skipped a passage, they probably won't believe you. This happens to our students all the time, and it's not surprising. But the truth is that, if your AJ friends doubt you, it's actually in your favor. Why? Because, on the ACT, whether you like it or not, it's you against everyone else, and if they continue to use the AJ approach, they'll continue to get AJ scores while you do better.

But what if everybody used this strategy? Fat chance. We could never get everyone to implement this strategy; remember, about a quarter of a million students take this test every time it is offered. Also, think about it: we could tell everyone that if they skip a passage, their scores would improve, but most people would tell us we're nuts. Isn't that how you reacted? We had to show you how this could work and make sure you knew that this strategy does not work unless you practice. Skipping the last passage does you no good if you don't do enough practice to get 14 out of 15 on the first four passages.

WHAT IF I ALREADY HAVE A 25 OR 26 ON THE ENGLISH SECTION AND NEED A HIGHER SCORE?

We hear this all the time, and we understand where you're coming from. Many colleges, and especially scholarships, are so competitive these days that you need a score at least in the upper 20s but usually 30 and above to be considered. So, let us tell you a story that will illustrate how we get our students to score even higher.

One of our students, Matt, came to us as a sophomore with a score of 20 on the English section. He listened to us, practiced, and applied our strategy exactly. He took the ACT at the end of his sophomore year and got a 26. When he told his friends that he skipped the last passage and still got a 26, they thought he was lying.

Matt was pleased with his score, but needed a higher one to get a scholarship to an out-of-state engineering school. He asked us how to modify the strategy to do better. Our answer: you don't. We did nothing differently; we just had him practice and do more and more practice tests.

Gradually, Matt found himself with more and more time at the end of the fourth passage. Why? It's true that he did acquire a great deal of knowledge about the ACT, but he also did so much practice that the test became somewhat repetitive and boring for him. He saw the same kinds of questions over and over, so he naturally got faster and faster. When he found himself with extra time, he would do just a few of the questions in the last passage and guess on the rest. Because he had been trained to perform at such high quality, he would get those extra questions right, just as he did in the first four passages.

The last time that Matt took the ACT was June of his junior year. After the test, he told us he had a little over eight minutes left when he finished the fourth passage. That's plenty of time to do the last passage and to do it with the same quality as the first four passages.

Now before we tell you how Matt did, let's consider what that would mean hypothetically. If he got 14 out of 15 on all five passages, that would have been 70 questions correct out of 75. On ACT test form 0661C, he would have gotten a score of 33.

What happened to Matt? He ended up scoring a 35 on the English section, which means he must have gotten 15 out of 15 correct on some of the passages. How did that happen? We've seen it time and again. It's all a matter of practice. Start by skipping a passage, practice, practice, practice, and follow the strategy. Eventually, if you spend enough time practicing, you will get to the point where the last passage is added back and the same high quality applied to it as in the first four passages. In time, the questions on the test become so boring that you may start getting all 15 questions correct on some of the passages, but that will be because of your hard work and practice, not because of us.

Now, be careful! We sometimes see students who get super excited about our strategy and incorrectly view it as a way to magically get a better score without having to practice. For them, the strategy can backfire because they skip the last passage but don't back it up with the quality needed in the first four passages. For more on how to prevent this from happening, take a look at our FAQs.

DO I HAVE ENOUGH TIME TO PRACTICE?

Those of you who picked up this book a month, a week, or even the day before the ACT are probably wondering if you can even use this strategy since you don't have time to practice. This is a valid concern. As we mentioned, practice is absolutely critical to carrying out this strategy, so we would **strongly** recommend that you take the ACT again, if possible. That way, you'll have more time to practice, and the more practice the better.

That being said, even if you are taking the ACT tomorrow, you should still apply the basis of this strategy. While we don't recommend that you skip a passage, we do recommend that you focus on quality over quantity, which will help you improve your score. For example, if you get to a question that you think you just need an extra 30 seconds to get right, spend those 30 seconds and try to get the answer correct.

But don't be disappointed that you learned about this strategy too close to the test. Instead, be happy that you know about it at all. Just use the opportunity to plan to retake the test and really prepare for it.

In summary: practice, practice, practice, take your time on the first four passages in the English section, and guess on every question in the last passage. If you practice enough that you find yourself with time at the end of the fourth passage, do whatever number of questions that you can in the last passage while still maintaining high quality and guessing on the rest.

The bottom line is that this strategy can be your ticket out of the AJ zone, and it can prepare you for whatever score you need on the ACT as long as you invest the necessary time and discipline into implementing it.

Chapter 6
Math

You've seen how our strategy is applied to the English section. Now we'll show you how to apply it to the Math section.

First, let's further develop our mental map. What do we know about the Math section? We know that there are 60 questions for which we have 60 minutes.

BAD testtakers TIP

Hopefully, you're updating your *BTT Mental Map* as you move through this book. Remember, this sheet will help you to really cement the strategy in your mind. If you need another copy, you can find one on our website, BadTestTakers.com, under *Resources*.

1. English

75 Questions
45 Minutes

2. Math

60 Questions
60 Minutes

3. Reading

4. Science

*Based on the Raw Score Conversion Table of ACT Test Form 0661C (page 63)

We talked about the "one minute per question" standard for evaluating the fairness of a test section and decided that it was arbitrary. On the Math section, we have an average of one minute per question. So, does that make it fair? It depends. There will be some questions that probably only take 30 seconds or less, some that may take about a minute, and quite a few that might take even longer. We are of the opinion that the time limit on this section is almost fair. We think that even adding five minutes would make the Math section much more fair, but we don't make the rules.

The Math section also has two big structural differences from the English, Reading, and Science sections. The other three sections have only four answer options per question and are broken into passages. The Math has five answer options per question and is not broken into passages; there are simply 60 questions.

2. Math

60 Questions

60 Minutes

★ No passages

Right now, we hope you're thinking: *how can we skip a passage in the Math section like we did in the English section, if there are no passages?* If that's what you were thinking, well done! You're well on your way to *shaking off* that AJ programming. If not, stay with us. You'll get the hang of it soon enough.

The fact that the Math section is not divided into parts or passages is, in fact, bad for us because it doesn't work with our previous strategy. But before we get too worried about that, let's talk about another unique feature of the Math section: its increasing level of difficulty. Grab one of your ACT test forms and flip through the Math section. You'll notice that the kind of math required by the questions tends to get progressively tougher and less familiar as you move through those 60 questions.

We can use this added feature to our advantage. How? Well, there aren't built-in points in the Math section where the questions switch from easy to medium to hard, so we're just going to make them up. We're going to split the Math section into three "passages" of 20 questions. And, since the level of difficulty increases as you progress through the test, we'll call questions 1 through 20 the "easy" questions, 21 through 40 the "medium" questions, and 41 through 60 the "hard" questions.

Are these "passages" real? Nope. Does the level of difficulty jump from easy to medium after question number 20? Not really. It's actually more gradual than that, but who cares? We're not doing research on the ACT; we're trying to perform better on it. And viewing the Math section in this simplified but strategic way will do exactly that: it will give you an advantage over all of the AJs who see the Math section as a big, dreadful block of who knows how many questions that must be answered frantically in order to finish before time is called.

2. Math

60 Questions

60 Minutes

★ No passages
★ Level of difficulty →

EASY	MEDIUM	HARD
1 - 20	21 - 40	41 - 60
20	20	20

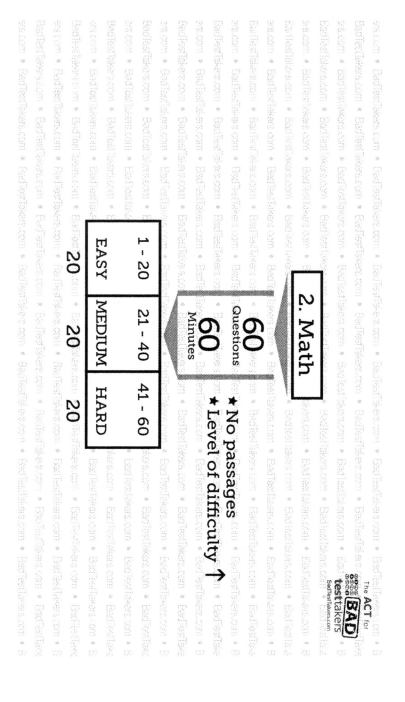

What do we teach our students to do? Unlike the AJs, our students focus on quality instead of quantity, which means we start by sacrificing a passage in order to get more time. So, which passage do you want to skip? Of course you want to skip the hard questions. Happily, those are the ones we want you to skip too. There are three good reasons that you should skip the "hard passage" on the Math section.

The first reason is that you're more likely to already have or more easily acquire the knowledge needed for the easy and medium questions than you are the hard questions.

Second, the hard questions generally take more time than the easy and medium do. We mentioned earlier the benefit of focusing on quality over quantity and why it is worth sacrificing questions in order to gain more time to answer other questions correctly. If we sacrifice the last 20 questions, we are not only getting more time for the first 40 questions, but we're also eliminating the questions that would have taken the most time if we had decided to do them.

Lastly, remember that question number 1 and question number 60 are worth exactly the same amount. While the difficulty level increases, the amount that the questions are worth does not. So, it makes more sense to spend the time necessary to minimize careless errors on the easy and medium questions than to spend a ton of time struggling with the hard questions.

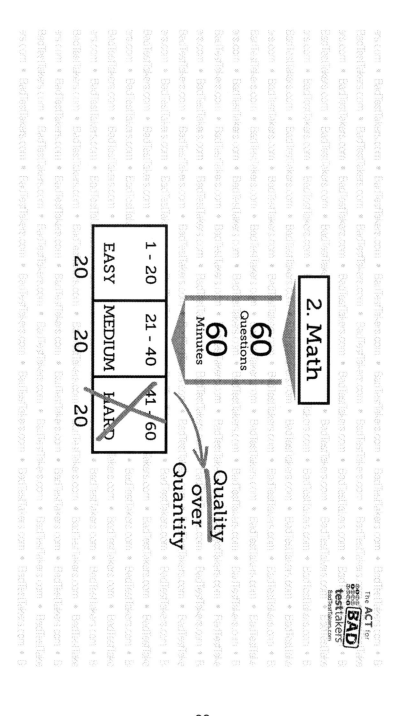

2. Math

60 Questions
60 Minutes

1 - 20	21 - 40	41 - 60
EASY	MEDIUM	HARD
20	20	20

Quality over Quantity

While on the English section we expect you to get 14 out of 15 correct in each passage, we don't expect you to get 19 out of 20 in the first "passage" of the Math section. Instead, we expect you to get all 20!

We know. That sounds really harsh. But we called it the "easy passage" for a reason. The kind of math that shows up in the first 20 questions tends to be arithmetic (often in word problems), basic algebra (e.g., solving simple equations and how to find things like slope and midpoint), and some very basic geometry (e.g., questions testing perimeter, area, and the number of degrees in a line or triangle).

[BAD] testtakers TIP

The ACT is really good at making the first 20 questions on the Math section seem harder than they really are. Don't be fooled! For example, try question #15 on page 27 of ACT test form 0661C. Go ahead. We'll wait.

Well, what do you have to do to get that one right? Just count the squares! I bet you didn't think it was going to test your ability to count when you first read it. Always remind yourself that if it's in the first 20 questions, it is easy.

Now, just because it's the "easy" passage, doesn't mean you'll automatically be able to get all 20 questions right. You may have forgotten some of this math, or maybe you were never taught it properly. Or, maybe you're the kind of test taker who moves too quickly and makes a lot of careless errors. Or, maybe you just hate math and have a lot of anxiety when confronted with a math question. All of those situations are understandable, but they can all be addressed through practice.

We expect 20 correct answers because we think you can do it, and our students have consistently shown us that this is the case. If you get 17 questions correct instead of 20 on the "easy" passage, it's not the end of the world, and the strategy doesn't collapse. But you need to go back, look at the three you missed, and try to understand why. In most cases, our students want to kick themselves when they see what they did wrong.

[BAD]testtakers'TIP

Here's an example. Take a look at #11 in the Math section of ACT test form 0661C. This is a trickier question than it may seem at first. Some students get this wrong because they square 3x and then square 7 to get answer choice C. Students who remember their algebra from school will correctly expand the expression to (3x+7)(3x+7) and FOIL to arrive at the correct answer choice, E.

But, even if you forgot your algebra rules, here's another way to do it. The question says "For all x." That means that x can be anything. So let's just say x is 1 and plug that into the original. That gives us 3 times 1, which is 3. Add 7, which gives us 10. Square that and we get 100. So, the answer is 100 when x is 1. Now, we just have to go through the choices and find which one says 100. We can do this very quickly. A and B both give us 20 if we substitute 1 for x, C gives us 58, D gets closer with 79, but E gives us 100.

Your calculator can help you do this more efficiently, and it usually takes less time than "FOILing." But no matter how you choose to tackle this question, there's really no good reason to get it wrong.

In our content-based book, we show you a powerful but little-known method to solve this problem and many like it extremely quickly using your calculator.

We're much nicer when it comes to the medium difficulty questions. We only ask that you get 15 out of those 20. Those problems normally include somewhat tougher algebra problems, tougher geometry problems, and some basic trigonometry.

Fifteen out of 20 is not easy, and it takes a lot of practice; that's why we're only asking you to get 15. But don't assume that getting 15 out of 20 questions correct won't take practice. It will.

On the last "passage," we expect you to guess on all of the questions. Unfortunately, in the Math section, your option choices have increased to five, so your odds of guessing correctly are 20%. That means that if you are guessing on 20 questions, you can expect to get four correct.

Why do the makers of the ACT give you five answer choices in the Math section but only four in the other three sections? It definitely lowers your odds of guessing correctly, but why would they only want to do that in the Math section?

Here's our theory: the Math section is the portion of the ACT in which you have the greatest ability to use the answer choices against the test. In short, you can plug and chug, estimate, etc. They know you have a calculator and a set number of choices, so, on some questions, you can simply start testing answer choice after answer choice. That's not something you can really do in the Reading section. The makers of the ACT know this, so they add an extra answer choice to each question to slow you down and make it less likely that you will guess correctly.

If you follow our strategy, you will have 20 correct answers in the first "passage," 15 correct in the second, and 4 correct in the third. Thus, you would have a total of 39 questions correct in the Math section. According to page 63 of ACT test form 0661C, having 39 correct answers in the Math section would yield a score of 25.

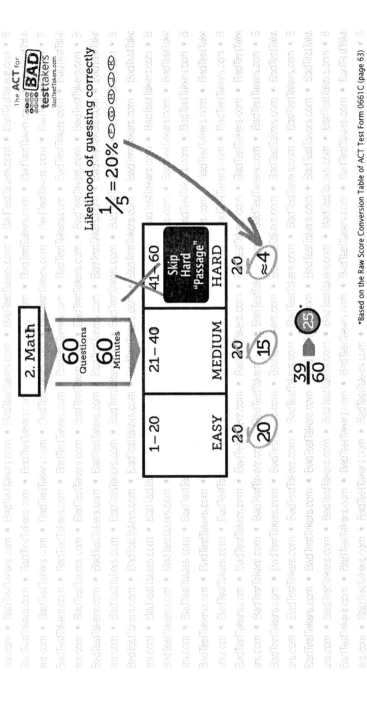

Likelihood of guessing correctly

$$\tfrac{1}{5} = 20\%$$

*Based on the Raw Score Conversion Table of ACT Test Form 0661C (page 63)

If you're willing to make a long-term commitment to improving your ACT score, our strategy has the ability to boost your score even higher. We see it in our students all the time. How does this happen on the Math section? After months of practice, you'll begin to notice that answering many of these questions becomes repetitive and boring to you so that you gradually have more time left after you finish question 40. Then, you can spend that extra time working at least a few of the questions in the "hard passage" in the same high-quality manner. If you practice enough, you'll eventually get to the point where you are answering all or most of the 60 questions in the time allotted, but in a high-quality way rather than in a rushing, AJ-style way.

As in the English section, those of you who picked up this book a month, a week, or the day before the ACT are probably wondering if you can even use this strategy since you don't have time to practice. This is a valid concern. First, we would **strongly** recommend that you plan to retake the ACT, if possible. That way you'll give yourself more time to practice, and the more practice, the better.

That being said, even if you are taking the ACT tomorrow, you should still apply the essence of our strategy. While we don't recommend that you skip the last 20 questions, we do recommend that you focus on quality over quantity, which will help you improve your score, even if you don't end up finishing the whole section.

For example, if you get to a question that you think you just need an extra 30 seconds on, spend those 30 seconds and try to get the answer correct, and be extra careful in the beginning of the Math section where the questions are easier. So many test takers feel so pressured to finish the test that they make mistakes on easy questions they know how to do, just so they can spend the last 20 minutes of the test working on questions they don't even understand. What sense does that make?

In summary: practice, practice, practice, take your time on the first 40 questions in the Math section, and guess on every single one of the last 20 questions. If you practice enough that you find yourself with time after finishing question 40, that's great! Every additional question you manage to get right will just raise your score. Do whatever number of questions that you can while still maintaining high quality and guessing on the rest.

Chapter 7
Reading

Ok, so you've seen how our strategy is applied to the English and Math sections. Now we'll show you how to apply it to the Reading section.

BAD testtakers TIP

On test day, you'll be given a "short break" between the Math and Reading sections. Usually, it's about ten to fifteen minutes long. Check out the FAQ at the end of this book for tips on how to use this break strategically.

BAD testtakers TIP

When you sum up the time allotted for the four sections of the ACT, the total testing time comes to 2 hours and 55 minutes. However, when you add in the break and the time needed for the proctor to distribute the test, read instructions, and walk you through completing the form, the entire test amounts to about four hours. So, if you're not taking the optional 30-minute writing test offered by the ACT, you should expect to end around noon.

Because the test is so long, we recommend you do some conditioning and build up your stamina. We answer an FAQ at the end of this book with our suggestions on how to do this.

Again, we need to begin our analysis of the Reading section by further developing our mental map. (By the way, make sure you're still taking notes by updating this information on your *BTT Mental Map.*) What do we know about the format of the Reading section? We know that there are 40 questions for which we have 35 minutes.

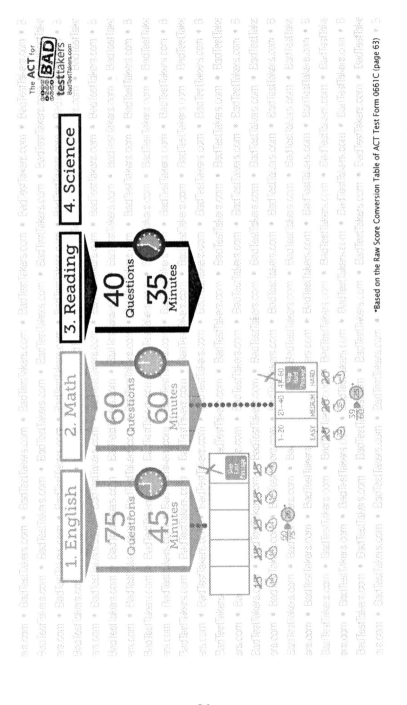

The ACT for **BAD** testtakers

BadTestTakers.com

1. English
75 Questions
45 Minutes

2. Math
60 Questions
60 Minutes

3. Reading
40 Questions
35 Minutes

4. Science

*Based on the Raw Score Conversion Table of ACT Test Form 0661C (page 63)

We talked about the "one minute per question" standard and decided that it was arbitrary. What about the ACT's time constraint on the Reading section? Is it fair? In our opinion, it's not. In fact, we think this is the most unfair section on the ACT in terms of timing. Let's take a closer look and see why.

The 40 questions are divided into four passages. Each passage contains about a page of text and ten questions.

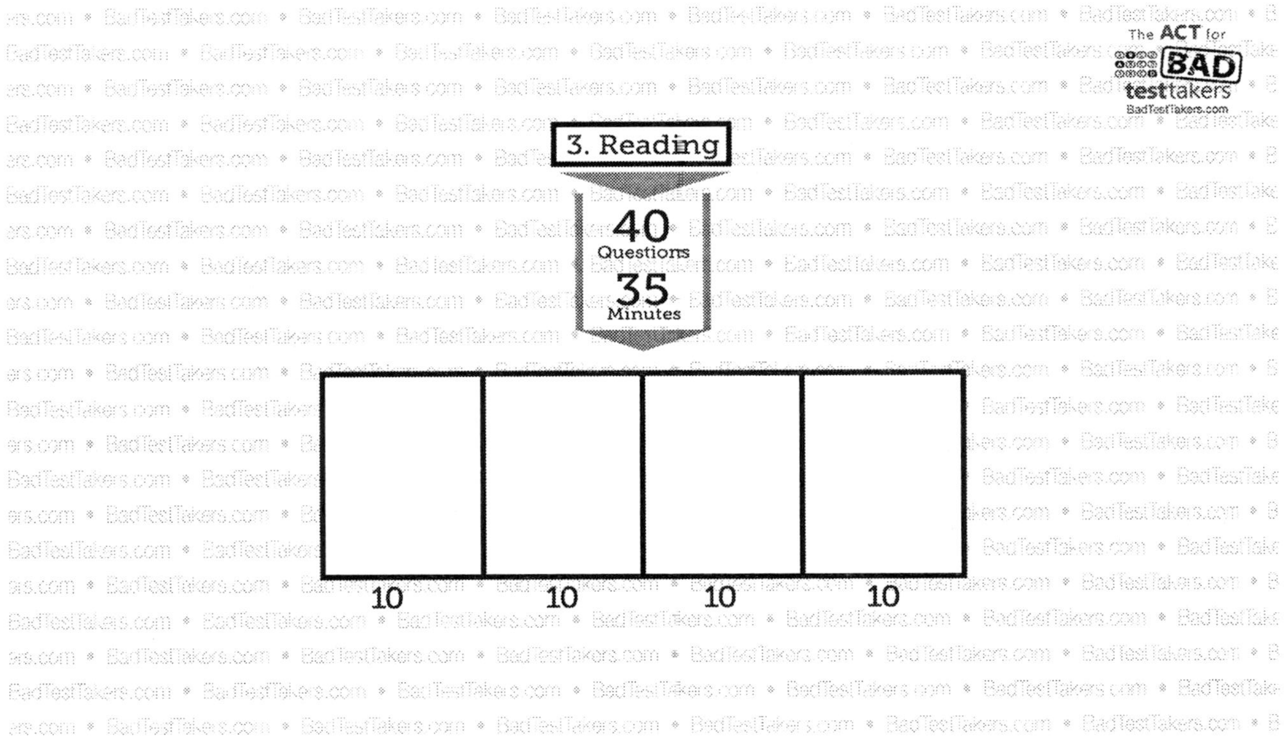
The ACT for BAD testtakers
BadTestTakers.com
3. Reading
40
Questions
35
Minutes
10
10
10
10

We know that we only get 35 minutes, but let's pretend that there are actually 36 minutes. We know that's not actually the case, but it will make the math easier. Dividing 36 minutes by four, you get nine minutes to complete each passage. But we actually have a little *less* than nine minutes on average per passage (because we really have 35 minutes, not 36).

Now, take a look at one of the passages in the Reading section on ACT test form 0661C, which starts on page 34. How long do you think it would take you just to read one of those? We think the average American high school student needs roughly five minutes to read a passage, leaving less than four minutes to answer all ten questions about that passage. That seems really unfair! And that doesn't even factor in the time you'll need to bubble in your answers.

However, while there are many students who agree with us that the timing is unfair, there are always some students who tell us that the Reading section doesn't really give them any problems and that they just naturally do very well on that section. What we have found is that these students are "readers." They read for fun, and they've made a habit of reading for most of their lives, so they read relatively quickly. These students aren't as affected by the time constraint on this section, because, in essence, they started preparing for the Reading section of the ACT when they were very young – they just didn't know it.

If you're one of these students, you have a great advantage that will really serve you on the Reading section of the ACT. If you're not, don't worry. You can still develop your reading efficiency through practice. For now, let's show you how we suggest you tackle this section.

We mentioned earlier that the Reading section has four passages of ten questions each. For those of you who have been paying attention or taking notes, we bet most of you think we're going to tell you to skip the last passage. You're half right. We do want you to skip a passage, but it isn't necessarily the last one that should be skipped. So which one do you skip? The shortest? The longest?

The passages that the ACT uses for the Reading section are divided by content. There are four categories of passages in the Reading section, and there is always one of each category on the test in exactly the same order. The categories, in order, are Prose Fiction, Social Science, Humanities, and Natural Science.

Prose Fiction is just a passage from a fictional story. Social Science could cover a number of topics, such as history, geography, anthropology, political science, psychology, sociology, and economics. The Humanities passage covers topics like art, music, dance, theater, philosophy, architecture, film, literature, and poetry. The Natural Science passage will contain topics about chemistry, physics, biology, anatomy, cosmology, geology, astronomy, and the like.

Content of the Passages

3. Reading

Prose Fiction	Social Science	Humanities	Natural Science
Story/ Narrative	History, Geography, Anthropology, Political Science, Psychology, Sociology, Economics, etc.	Art, Music, Dance, Theater, Philosophy, Architecture, Film, Literature, Poetry, etc.	Biology, Chemistry, Geology, Cosmology, Astronomy, Physics, Anatomy, etc.
10	10	10	10

So, should you pick the "skip passage" based on topic? No, we don't think so. However, we do think it's important that you know what you're up against, and knowing the passage types and the topics they cover can be helpful. You also can't skip the boring passage. Chances are, you'll think they're all boring, so that idea doesn't help you much.

So how do you know which passage to skip? We want you to skip a passage based on the level of difficulty with which it is written. We know that sounds really vague, but if you take a look at a practice ACT, or better yet five or more, you will see what we mean.

The method we recommend is to keep in your mind that you have a "Get Out of This Passage" card, and start by giving the Prose Fiction the benefit of the doubt. In other words, when time starts, just begin by reading the first passage as if you're not planning to skip anything. After the first paragraph, stop and ask yourself if you understood what you read. Of course it's going to be boring, but that's not the issue. The issue is whether you read it once and understood it. If it makes sense and you understand what it's about, keep reading; that isn't the passage you should skip.

But, if you did not understand it and you would need to reread the paragraph, skip that passage. We showed you how little time we have on this section. There's not a lot of time to reread paragraphs and struggle with complicated sentences, so as soon as you find the passage with a first paragraph that seems difficult to understand, skip that passage and move on to the next one.

Let's try this out. Read the first paragraph of each passage in the Reading section of ACT test form 0661C (page 34) and come back with the one you think should be skipped. Go ahead. We'll wait.

The ACT for
BAD
testtakers

Well, which one would you have skipped? If you think it's Passage III, we agree. That passage is much tougher to read than the others. So, here, it would have been wise to have skipped it.

[BAD] testtakers' TIP

Every once in a while, there is a test with two really difficult passages instead of just one. Don't panic! If there are two hard passages, the curve is likely to work in your favor because the section is harder. Just pick one to do and skip the other one.

Finding the skip passage in ACT test form 0661C turned out to be pretty easy, but that's not always the case. The ability to identify the skip passage takes time and practice to develop. The skill of spotting which passage is unusually hard only starts to show up once you've practiced through about three Reading sections (or about 12 passages). At that point, you start to become familiar with the ACT's passages, and you have a good sense of whether or not a passage is more difficult than usual.

[BAD] testtakers' TIP

We always have students who ask whether they should really *read* the passage or just *skim*. You should definitely *read* it. As a general rule, you should not just skim; you're skipping one of the passages precisely so that you can have extra time to actually *read* and really understand the passage well. There is, however, one exception to this rule, which we'll discuss in a later TIP box. For now, know that you should actually *read* the passages carefully. Remember, it's all about quality over quantity.

Note that whether a passage should be skipped is not dependent upon vocabulary. If you see a word you do not know, that doesn't necessarily mean that you should skip that passage. First, try using context to see if you more or less understand what the word likely means, but if you still can't figure it out, then just cross it out and move on.

If you don't have time to hone the skill of identifying the skip passage or have trouble spotting it on test day, don't lose time – just do the first three and skip the last passage.

[BAD]testtakers TIP

By the way, if it's tough for you to even do three passages in the time allotted, we understand. The Reading and Science are the most aggressively timed sections of the ACT. But don't get discouraged. Just keep practicing. While we've definitely seen our share of students not put in the work, we've also never had a disciplined student who put in the work and didn't improve on this section.

As with the English and Math sections, we expect you to take the additional time you have by eliminating a passage to produce high-quality work on the other three passages. With your extra time gained by reducing the number of questions from 40 to 30, we expect you to get nine out of the ten questions on each of the three passages that you complete. That's not an easy task; it requires a lot of practice on real ACT passages.

As for the skip passage, you are just going to guess on every question like you did for the passages we skipped on the English and Math sections. Like the English section, you have four answer options per question and one correct answer; that means you can expect to guess correctly 25% of the time. Out of the 10 questions on the skip passage, you will most likely guess correctly on either two or three, but let's say you're having a bad guessing day and only get two. Taken together, that would give you a total of 29 questions correct out of 40.

According to page 63 of ACT test form 0661C, that would yield a score of 27. Based on our experience, that's a bit high because of the test form we are using. Normally, our strategy will yield a score between 24 and 26. A score of 27 probably means that this Reading section was harder than usual, so fewer test takers managed to answer 29 questions correctly than normally occurs.

To compare, let's take a look at a different test form. Open up ACT test form 1267C. The table on page 61 shows that 29 questions correct out of 40 on that test takers generally found the Reading section would yield a score of 24. That basically means that test takers generally found the Reading section on this test easier than the one in 0661C. In other words, getting 29 questions out of 40 wasn't as tough to do on 1267C and so deserves a 24 instead of a 27.

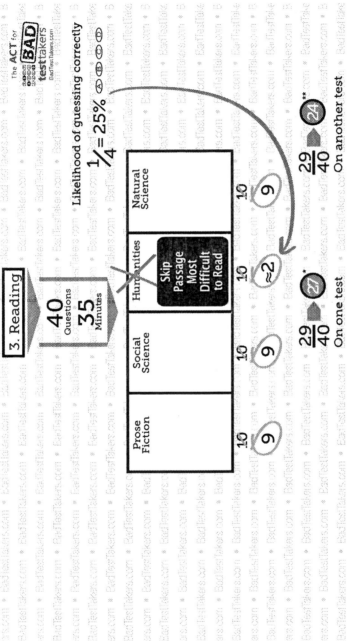

The ACT for **BAD** testtakers
BadTestTakers.com

3. Reading

40 Questions
35 Minutes

Prose Fiction	Social Science	Humanities	Natural Science

Skip Passage Most Difficult to Read

Prose Fiction: 10 → 9
Social Science: 10 → 9
Humanities: 10 → ≈2
Natural Science: 10 → 9

*Likelihood of guessing correctly

$\frac{1}{4} = 25\%$ Ⓐ Ⓑ Ⓒ Ⓓ

$\frac{29}{40}$ → **27** *   On one test

$\frac{29}{40}$ → **24** **   On another test

*Based on the Raw Score Conversion Table of ACT Test Form 0661C (page 63)   **Based on the Raw Score Conversion Table of ACT Test Form 1267C (page 61)

Is it possible to score even higher on the the Reading section using this strategy? With time and practice, yes. Going through a lot of practice Reading sections eventually makes you more efficient at reading the passages and answering the questions correctly. Gradually, you'll find yourself with a little more time left over after you finish the third passage. When that happens, you can spend that time doing what you can on the skipped passage. Even if you only manage to get one or two more questions right in the skip passage, it often translates to a higher score.

BAD testtakers TIP

Earlier, we said we didn't want you to skim. However, if you finish the three passages that you didn't skip and have, say, three minutes left, we don't expect you to sit there and do nothing. At the same time, it doesn't make sense to start reading the skip passage when you know you won't finish it and have time to answer any of the questions.

So what should you do? Before looking at the text, we recommend you look for questions that reference line numbers. The easiest ones are those that ask about the meaning of a specific word and give you a line number. These can be spotted quickly because the word is usually *italicized* in the question.

For example, take a look at questions 36 and 37 in the Reading section of ACT test form 1267C (page 41). On questions like these, you can use your remaining time to go to the line indicated and start reading carefully. But don't just read that line; start with the sentence before it and read until the sentence after it to give yourself some context. That's usually enough information to answer these kinds of questions.

If you aren't lucky enough to have any of those questions in your skip passage, find another question with line numbers, but preferably one asking about a short number of lines (one or two is best) and try to answer that question instead.

As with the previous sections, those of you who picked up this book a month, a week, or the day before the ACT are probably wondering if you can even use this strategy since you don't have time to practice. That's very tough to do, especially with the Reading section.

As usual, we would first **strongly** advise you to consider taking the ACT at least one more time. That way, you have more time to practice this strategy, and the more practice the better.

That being said, even if you are taking the ACT tomorrow, you should still apply the idea behind this strategy. While we don't recommend that you skip a passage, we do recommend that you focus on quality over quantity, which will help you improve your score. For example, if you get to a question that asks about something you remember reading about in the passage and just need an extra 30 seconds to find the answer in the text, spend those 30 seconds and try to get the answer correct, even if it means not getting to every question.

THE ISSUE OF OUTSIDE KNOWLEDGE

This a good place to stop to talk about how the ACT designs their sections. The English and Math sections require you to bring your knowledge into the test. In the English section, the ACT is not going to give you a question involving a semi-colon and also give you an explanation of what a semicolon does and how to use it. If you don't know that, you're in trouble. That's why practice is key. You need to learn that outside knowledge and bring it into the test with you. Likewise, in the Math section, the ACT is not going to give you a word problem where you need to find the area of a circle and also tell you that the area of a circle is equal to πr^2. One of the purposes of such a question is to test whether you already know that or not. On the English and Math sections, you're expected to rely on knowledge that you learned in school or in your practice sessions to answer the questions correctly.

The Reading section, on the other hand, just requires that you have the ability to read and understand English. That is all. Now, the ACT doesn't give you very much time to do that, but everything you need in order to answer the questions is contained within the passage. So, taking the extra time to do the questions in the three passages you don't skip is really worthwhile. Why? Because the only thing you need to do with that extra time is look through the passage. You don't have to try to remember rules or formulas; you just have to look through the text and find the answer to each question. Sometimes, you'll remember the answer from your reading. But even if you don't, you usually at least recall where, generally, in the text that topic was discussed.

But be careful! The makers of the ACT are aware that they have to give you the answers in the passage. So, in order to make the Reading section challenging, they hide the answers in a massive amount of text, use questions that are confusingly worded, and use subtle tricks within the wrong answer choices to make them more appealing. As if that wasn't enough, they severely limit the amount of time they give you so that you rush and become more prone to making careless errors. Taking your time and doing high-quality work is essential to doing well on the Reading section because outside knowledge isn't going to help you.

In summary: practice, practice, practice, take your time on the three passages you actually do in the Reading section, and guess on every question in the skip passage. If you practice enough that you find yourself with time after completing three passages, by all means, move on to the skip passage. Do whatever number of questions that you can in the skip passage (that's where skimming can come in handy) while still maintaining high quality and guessing on the rest.

Chapter 8
Science

In many ways, the Science section seems like another Reading section. Let's start with format. Just like the Reading section, the Science section also gives you 35 minutes to complete 40 questions. You might think that's just a coincidence, but we don't think so.

[BAD] testtakers TIP

Remember to keep taking notes with your *BTT Mental Map*. If you need another copy, you can find it on our website, BadTestTakers.com, under *Resources*.

Like the Reading section, the Science section does not heavily rely on outside knowledge. That's always hard for some of our students to accept, but it is absolutely true. Since both the Reading and Science sections do not focus their questions on outside knowledge, it makes sense to us that the ACT would make the two sections similar in structure.

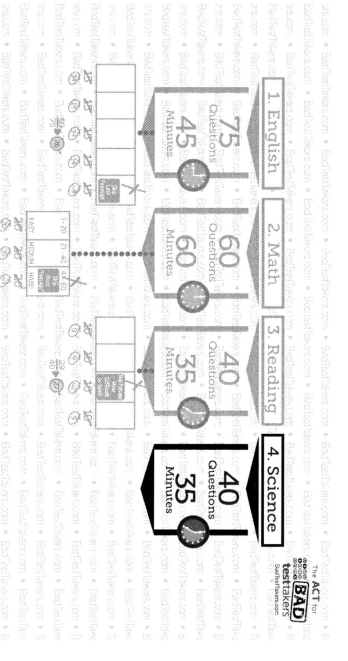

1. English
75 Questions
45 Minutes

2. Math
60 Questions
60 Minutes

3. Reading
40 Questions
35 Minutes

4. Science
40 Questions
35 Minutes

*Based on the Raw Score Conversion Table of ACT Test Form 0661C (page 63)

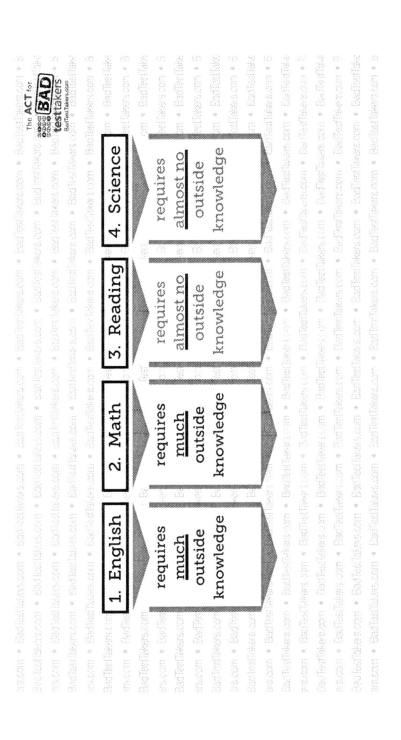

1. English — requires <u>much</u> outside knowledge

2. Math — requires <u>much</u> outside knowledge

3. Reading — requires <u>almost no</u> outside knowledge

4. Science — requires <u>almost no</u> outside knowledge

The Science section, however, has seven passages instead of four like the Reading section. Given that seven does not divide into 40 evenly, we discover another unique aspect of the Science section: some of its passages have more questions than others.

Flipping through the pages of a Science section reveals that each passage has between five and seven questions. But, in studying the format, we've noticed a few more things about the Science section. For example, there are always three passages that have *five* questions, three passages that have *six* questions, and one passage that has *seven* questions, although not necessarily in that order.

4. Science

40 Questions

35 Minutes

7	6	6	5	5	6	5

Before we launch into passages and determining which one to skip, let's talk a little bit about content. Basically, there are four ways the ACT presents you with information in any passage of the Science section: graphs, text, tables (or charts), and diagrams (or pictures).

Two of these you should like, and the other two, you shouldn't. You should definitely *like* graphs and tables. You should *dislike* text and pictures.

[BAD] testtakers TIP

Very often on the ACT there is a passage in the Science section with one unconventional graph or chart. Don't freak out! We know they look weird, but they are usually not as difficult to read as they seem, so don't let them scare you. Just be patient with them. Take your time to figure them out. If you want examples, take a look at the last passage of the Science section in ACT test form 0661C (page 54) and the last passage of ACT test form 1267C (page 53). (By the way, it won't always be on the last passage. We checked.)

Science: It's All about Knowing Where to Look

- **Graphs**

- **Text**

- **Tables**
  (Charts)

- **Diagrams**
  (Pictures)

There are two reasons you should focus on graphs and tables instead of text and diagrams: (1) it is much easier and quicker to retrieve information from graphs and tables than from text and diagrams, and (2) the answers to the questions on the Science section are *most often* located in graphs and tables.

We teach our students to focus on the graphs and tables of the Science section much more than on its text and pictures. Are the answers to the questions ever in the text and pictures? Yes, but not often enough that you should concentrate your efforts on them. In fact, they usually just serve to confuse students and to make them think that outside knowledge is important. We've seen many passages where the text and the pictures turn out to be completely unnecessary for correctly answering the questions. So, why are they there? They're effective in making the Science section of the ACT more challenging, because they do a good job of scaring test takers and wasting their limited time.

Science: It's All about Knowing Where to Look

- **Graphs**
- ~~Text~~
- **Tables** (charts)
- ~~Diagrams (pictures)~~

Why you should like graphs & tables:

- Easier & quicker to retrieve information
- Answers are most often found there

Why you should dislike text & pictures:

- Difficult & time-consuming to retrieve information
- Answers are much less often found there
- Often confusing & unnecessary

So, what do we propose? Do *not* read the text. That's right! Don't read the experiments. We know that's tough to do, especially when the questions sound so technical and you don't understand what they're saying. But believe us. Most of the time, you don't need to understand the science behind the passage. Usually, you just need to read a graph or a table. So don't read the text. It is a waste of your time, and you are pressured for time on this section. Instead, go to the questions immediately. Use each question to determine which graph and/or table it's asking about. The question usually tells you, but even if it doesn't, identify **landmarks** (see TIP box) in the question and in the answer choices, and then use them to locate the information you need to answer the question correctly.

BAD testtakers TIP

Unfortunately, sometimes the answers to Science questions are found in the text or in a picture. But that does not mean you should begin reading the experiment. Instead, *skim* the text and look for what we call **landmarks**, which include (1) numbers, (2) scientific units, (3) technical-sounding words, (4) acronyms, and (5) italicized words. Landmarks really intimidate AJs, but they're actually very helpful in finding answers, and they're easy to spot when you're skimming, so get comfortable locating and using them to your advantage.

By the way, there is one other thing that shows up from time to time in the Science section: equations, either chemical or mathematical. When they show up, they are almost always used on one question or another. They are usually easy to apply. When you spot an equation (even if it's in one of the questions), expect to apply it on at least one of the questions.

Now, knowing all that, let's get back to the passages and applying the strategy. When selecting which passage to skip, look for the passage that has no graphs or tables. There is usually only one passage that has just text or just text with pictures. In such a passage, the answers can't be in a graph or table because there aren't any! Because this passage will usually be more time-consuming, you don't want to deal with it, and you skip it.

We said we wanted you to skip the passage without any graphs or tables, but how does that relate to the number of questions per passage? It seems like that ought to make a difference, especially since we brought it up. If your instincts tell you that you should skip a passage that has five questions, that's good. It shows that you're beginning to understand how this strategy works and how you can best use it. All things being equal, you should want to skip a passage with a low number of questions, because you're less likely to do well on a passage you skip and guess on. After all, look back at the English, Math, and Reading sections and take a look at how many questions you're likely to answer correctly when you just guess. Not many at all. But, while it is reasonable to want to skip a passage with five questions to cut your losses, there's more to the story.

It turns out that, practically every single time, the passage with seven questions is the passage with only text or with text and a picture. So, while it is logical to want to skip a passage with only five questions, the passage with seven questions is overwhelmingly likely to be the one that has no graphs or tables and that relies heavily on the text. So that's the one that you should skip – the one with seven questions.

BAD testtakers TIP

We have only ever seen one ACT test form where the seven-question passage had graphs and a different passage was the one that lacked graphs and tables. If this happens on your test, don't panic! We still want you to skip the passage with seven questions. Why? The passage with seven questions usually includes "conflicting viewpoints" of students or scientists, and it will, therefore, rely heavily on the text. That makes it more time-consuming. So, just stick to the strategy, and when in doubt, count the questions. If there are seven, skip it. You can always come back to it, if you finish the other six passages and have extra time. And if not, no biggie.

BAD testtakers TIP

In both the Science and the Reading sections, be very careful about your bubbling. Because you might be skipping passages at the beginning or in the middle of the section, you need to be especially careful to make sure you are bubbling the correct ovals for the correct questions. We have only ever had one student who got off track and made a bubbling mistake because he skipped a passage and didn't make a note of it. But it was fairly disastrous. His score on the Science section brought his entire composite score way down. Obviously, he had to retake the test, so just be careful.

Skipping the seven-question passage leaves you with six passages having a total of 33 questions. Like the other sections, in order to be able to skip a passage, you must do the questions in the remaining six passages with a high degree of quality. What does that mean? With our students, we have them practice until they miss no more than one question on each of the six passages they actually do. If you meet this goal and miss only one question per passage, you would answer a total of 27 questions correctly.

What about the seven-question skip passage? We guess, as usual. In the seven-question passage, because you have four answer options and one correct answer, you have a 25% chance of answering a question correctly, just like in the English and Reading sections. That means you can expect to answer one or two correctly, but it is more likely that you will get two correct. Adding these two correct guesses to the 27 questions from the other six passages gives us a total of 29 correct answers out of 40.

According to page 63 of ACT test form 0661C, 29 correct answers on the Science section yields a score of 24. Keep in mind that we normally expect our students to get a couple more questions correct, which would raise the score up to a 25 or 26, and with practice, you can do that too.

4. Science

40 Questions

35 Minutes

Likelihood of guessing correctly

$\frac{1}{4} = 25\%$ Ⓐ Ⓑ Ⓒ Ⓓ

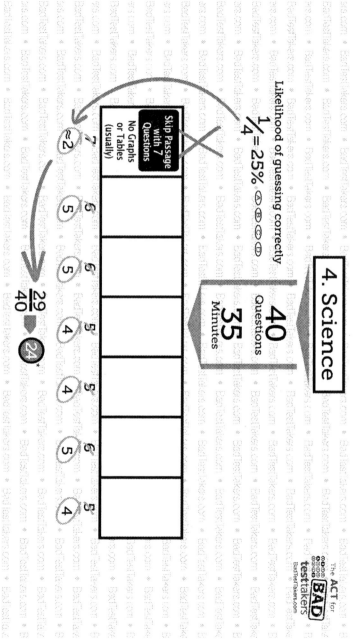

Skip Passage with 7 Questions					
No Graphs or Tables (usually)					
7	6	6	5	5	6
≈2	5	5	4	4	5
					5
					4

$\frac{29}{40}$ ➤ **24***

If your score in the Science section is already higher than 25, use the same strategy we talked about in all of the previous sections. That is, practice so much that answering these questions becomes second-nature so that you gradually have more time left after you finish the sixth passage. Then you can spend that time working on the skip passage in the same high-quality manner.

BAD testtakers TIP

If you finish the six passages you didn't skip and have just a few minutes left, just like in the Reading section, it would be a waste to sit there and just let the time run out. At the same time, since the seven-question passage has no graphs or tables, it doesn't make sense to start reading the skip passage when you know you won't finish it and have time to answer any of the questions.

So what should you do? Go to the first question and find its landmarks. Then, *skim* the passage looking for these landmarks. The answers are usually nearby. Even if you're only able to answer a question or two, every little bit helps. Just don't forget to leave enough time to guess on the questions you don't get to.

Once again, those of you who picked up this book a month, a week, or the day before the ACT are probably wondering if you can even use this strategy since you don't have time to practice. Of course, as you probably realize by now, this strategy cannot be implemented fully unless it is backed up by sufficient practice. For this reason, we **strongly** recommend that you consider taking the ACT again (and even a number of times more) so you can practice and successfully implement this approach. After all, the more practice the better.

That being said, even if you are taking the ACT tomorrow, you can still apply the basis of this strategy. While we don't recommend that you skip a passage, we do recommend that you focus on quality over quantity, which will help you improve your score. For example, if you get to a question that you think you just need an extra 30 seconds to find its answer on a graph, then we urge you to spend those 30 seconds and try to get the answer correct.

Remember that, while the English and Math sections require you to bring outside knowledge into the test with you, Science does not. Just about everything you need to answer the questions is contained within the passage (usually in the graphs and/or tables), which means that it is really worthwhile to take your time to carefully answer the questions in the six passages you complete. Why? Because the only thing you need to do with your time is find the graphs/tables containing the answer (or occasionally scan the text for the answer). You don't have to try to learn or remember scientific concepts or formulas; you just have to use landmarks to help you search through the information in the passage to find the answer to each question.

The problem is that, since the makers of the ACT will basically place almost all of the answers in front of you on the Science section, they need some way to make it challenging. So, they try to hide the answers to each question by confusing you with technical-sounding words, scientific acronyms, unconventional graphs, difficult text describing the experiment (which you don't need to read), and complicated pictures (which you should usually ignore). On top of that, they severely limit your time so that you are more prone to making careless errors. Taking your time and doing high-quality work is essential to doing well on the Science section.

1. English	2. Math	3. Reading	4. Science
requires <u>much</u> outside knowledge	requires <u>much</u> outside knowledge	requires almost no <u>outside</u> knowledge	requires almost no <u>outside</u> knowledge

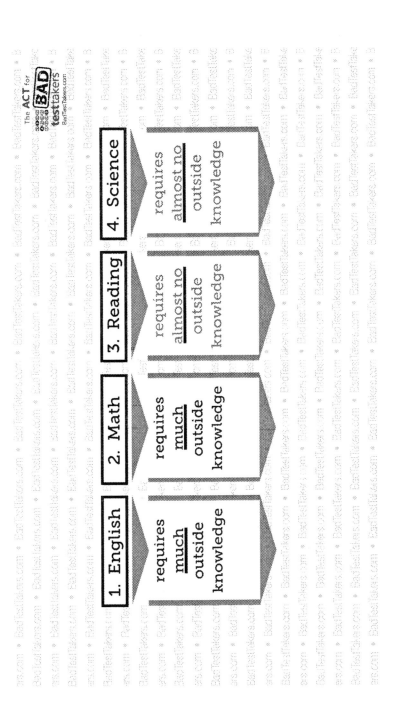

BAD testtakers TIP

Does the Science section ever test you on outside knowledge? Yes, but this happens so rarely that we suggest you ignore it. We have seen a few questions that depended on actual scientific knowledge (usually in biology), but these were never more than one or two per Science section. In the majority of cases, the outside knowledge needed is what most students consider common sense. Examples include knowing that gravity pulls objects downward, that higher density materials sink while lower density materials float, and that solids expand as they get warmer but contract as they get colder. Some of these may seem obvious to you, but, strictly speaking, they constitute outside knowledge. Your common sense knowledge of the world often proves useful on the Science section of the ACT, so make sure you use it.

To summarize, learn to take your time on the six passages you don't skip in the Science section, and guess on every question in the passage you do skip (the one with seven questions). Do as much practice as possible so that you develop the skill of finding the answers without reading the passages or really understanding what they're about. If you practice enough that you find yourself with time left over after you've completed the six passages, do whatever number of questions you can in the skip passage while still maintaining high quality and guessing on the rest.

Chapter 9
Bringing It All Together

We've devised an organized, practical attack plan for you to take into the ACT. While this strategy shocks many of our students at first, it later instills in them a renewed sense of hope about their future performance on the ACT. After reading this book, you may be feeling some newfound confidence about the test, and that's great! In fact, that's probably the most overlooked advantage to this strategy. But, now you must channel your confidence into discipline.

We've mentioned it many times, but it's worth repeating: in order for this strategy to work, it is absolutely critical that you practice. If you are taking the ACT in a month or less (especially if you're taking it tomorrow), we **strongly** recommend that you sign up to take the test again, if at all possible. Practice with actual retired ACT tests, at least five or six of them, and do some untimed followed by timed practice implementing the skip strategy in an environment similar to actual testing conditions. Review *all* of the questions, even the ones that you got right. That's the kind of practice that is necessary to fully benefit from this strategy.

Let's summarize. In the English section, skip the last passage and focus on the first four passages. Guess on the questions in the last passage.

In the Math, skip the last 20 questions and focus on the first 40 questions. Guess on the last 20 questions.

In the Reading passage, skip the passage that is the toughest to understand, and focus on the other three passages. Guess on the questions in the passage you skipped.

In the Science, skip the passage that has seven questions, and focus on the other six passages. Guess on the questions in the passage you skipped.

If you have done enough practice that you find yourself with extra time at the end of any of these sections, spend that extra time attempting as many questions as you can in the skip passage, but be sure to maintain the high quality you had for the questions you didn't skip. Even if you're only able to answer a question or two, every little bit helps. Just don't forget to leave enough time to guess on the questions you don't get to.

That's it. That's how you do well on the ACT, whether you are a bad test taker or not. And you're already well on your way to becoming a good test taker. If you aren't clear on the strategy and would like it presented in another way, check out our website at www.BadTestTakers.com. It includes the Crash Course videos that explain our strategy. If you are looking for some help with content, as we mentioned, our prep books on each section of the ACT will be coming out soon.

If you found this book helpful, please visit our website and let us know. We love to get feedback from our students.

Best of luck on the ACT!

Your New Mental Map of the ACT* ✏ Quality over Quantity!

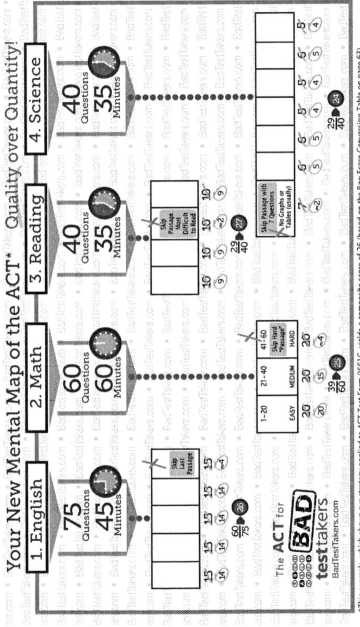

1. English
75 Questions
45 Minutes

Skip Last Passage

15 (14) 15 15 (14) 15 15 (14) (4)

60/75 ▶ 26

2. Math
60 Questions
60 Minutes

1-20	21-40	41-60
EASY	MEDIUM	Skip Hard "Passage" HARD
20 (20)	20 (15)	20 (4)

39/60 ▶ 25

3. Reading
40 Questions
35 Minutes

Skip Passage Most Difficult to Read

10" (9) 10" (9) 10 (9) 10" (9) 10" ≈2

29/40 ▶ 27

4. Science
40 Questions
35 Minutes

Skip Passage with Questions
No Graphs or Tables (usually)

6" (5) 6 (5) 5" (4) 7" ≈2 6" (5) 5" (4)

29/40 ▶ 24

The ACT for **BAD** testtakers
BadTestTakers.com

*This example, which shows our strategy applied to ACT Test Form 0661C, yields a composite score of 26 (based on the Raw Score Conversion Table on page 63). While raw score conversions vary among ACT Test Forms, our strategy typically yields a composite score of 25. More information is available on our website under *Resources*.

Chapter 10
The Best Kept Secret for Effective ACT Practice

Even though information about it is included on the ACT's website, few students, parents, and even teachers, counselors, and tutors seem to know about the Test Information Release (TIR). Out of the six administrations of the ACT each year, three (April, June, and December) include the option to order a TIR.

What is it? It is a service offered by the ACT that includes a copy of the test booklet from your administration along with an archaic-looking sheet[†] showing not only the correct answers to the test but also those you marked. This service currently costs an extra $19 that you can pay when you register for the ACT or can request up to three months after you took the test by completing a special order form. If you order the TIR, you'll get your official score report at the regular time (usually two to three weeks after the test), and the TIR information about three to four weeks after you receive your score report (about six weeks after the test).

---

†.   Apparently printed out from W.O.P.R.

BADtesttakers TIP

Links to more information about the TIR and to the TIR order form are available on our website, BadTestTakers.com, under *Resources*.

We simply cannot stress this enough: <u>always</u> order the TIR, especially since you should be expecting to take the ACT multiple times. In fact, we recommend that you sign up only for administrations when the TIR is available. For ACT tutors like us, the TIR is an extremely valuable tool because it allows us to evaluate whether our students actually implemented the strategy when they took the test. It also allows us to identify, for each student, the skills that need to be sharpened and the content that needs to be reviewed.

For test takers who are self-studying, the TIR is likewise a great resource; you can look over what you missed on the last test, identify problem areas, and plan a practice schedule that will allow you to get the most out of the remaining time you have before you retake the ACT.

How do we use the TIR to its greatest advantage? Let us tell you what we tell our students to do when they receive a TIR. When you get your TIR material, the first thing you should do is set aside a Saturday at 8 a.m. to retake the test. Yes. We know. You already took this test, and it would be torture to have to do it again. But, this is *so* necessary. You will probably repeat most of your mistakes and behavior, but that's what we're trying to find out: which questions you missed because of knowledge gaps and which questions you missed because of careless errors. After you retake it, grade it by going through the TIR answers and comparing what you got wrong the first time and the second time.

If you are not the super diligent type (which is fine), take your TIR packet to an experienced ACT tutor who can help you identify where to go from there. If nothing else, *at least* look at the questions you got wrong, redo those problems, and take the ones you don't understand to a tutor or a teacher with strong ACT experience.

The TIR is an incredibly valuable resource for test takers, and if you can manage to do it, you should try to take the ACT in April, June, or December every time you take it. That way, you'll be able not only to track your overall progress, but also to track your performance on questions that have historically given you trouble. Finally, the TIR is also a great way to get your hands on another *real* ACT test. Definitely take advantage of this awesome opportunity!

Part 2
Frequently Asked Questions

1. I love your strategy! I'm confident and motivated to get started. Now what?

Well, now you need to implement a practice plan.

First, review Chapter 2, which includes our suggestions on how to practice effectively. Next, you need to figure out how you are going to study. We recommend that our students start with a single section and practice it untimed. We ask them to start with the section they like the most or feel most comfortable with (or dread the least). So, let's say you are a science person. If you feel most at ease with the Science section, we would start by having you do untimed Science sections until you are successfully carrying out the strategy (in other words, only missing one question in each passage of the Science section). Once that happens, we would have you start doing timed Science sections and have you begin working on a different section untimed. Let's say English.

The pattern continues: once we see that you are adhering to the strategy (i.e., routinely getting 14 or 15 answers correct in each English passage), we would have you continue doing Science and English sections timed. We would also have you start practicing a new section untimed. Let's say Math.

Once you have the math strategy down and are routinely answering all of the first 20 questions and 15 of the middle 20 questions correctly, we would have you start doing timed Math sections, and add in Reading untimed. Finally, once you demonstrate that you are repeatedly getting nine out of ten questions correct on Reading passages, we would add Reading to your list of timed sections, thereby finishing out your practice with you doing whole timed tests.

An example of this practice plan is summarized in the table below for someone who chooses to start with the Science section.

	Start doing untimed sections when:	Strategic goal	Start doing timed sections when:
Science	Immediately	No more than one incorrect per passage	Goal is met
English	Science goal is met	14 out of 15 correct per passage	Goal is met
Math	English goal is met	20 out of 20 correct in the "easy passage" and 15 out of 20 correct in the "medium passage"	Goal is met
Reading	Math goal is met	9 out of 10 correct per passage	Goal is met
- Once all goals are met, start taking timed, full ACT practice tests.			

The idea of this table works for any arrangement of subjects you choose. If you want to start with Math and end with English, that's fine. However, the pattern ought to be the same: untimed until the goal is met, then timed, and add another untimed section until eventually you are doing complete, fully-timed practice tests.

2. How do I know that I'm ready to implement your strategy on the ACT?

This is our favorite question. The answer is that it becomes apparent in your practice sessions. After all, you can't really know if you're ready until you practice. Reading the strategy and having a mental map is key, but those things still need practice to be really useful. If you are not routinely getting the number of questions right that you need to get in order for the strategy to work, then you are not fully ready in that section. If you can't spot the difficult passage in the Reading section, you are not fully ready. If you can't reproduce your mental map of the ACT and the strategy on a blank piece of paper the night before the test, you are definitely not fully ready.

But, who said you had to be "fully ready" before going into the ACT? Unless it's the last time you ever plan to take the ACT, it's fine to go into the ACT not feeling fully ready. In fact, the ACT is the best kind of practice test for future ACTs. If you're not fully ready, just try applying the strategy as best you can and see what results you get. It will give you a good starting point for the next time that you take the ACT. Also, hopefully, you signed up for a TIR administration so you can order the TIR and really analyze what you did well and what you need to keep working on. (For more information on the TIR, see Chapter 10.

3. What if I'm taking the ACT tomorrow, and I just picked up this book?

Our approach is not a cram strategy. If you don't have enough time to practice, you won't fully be able to benefit from it. Therefore, we **strongly** recommend that you sign up to take the ACT again in a few months, if possible. After all, we would ideally like you to take the test at least three to five times, and we want you to have enough time to practice, get conditioned for the test, and become a great test taker.

If you're taking the test tomorrow and are just reading this now, you won't have time to practice implementing our strategy. Remember, you need practice to determine whether you're taking too long or still rushing. You need practice to be able to spot the hard passage in the Reading section. You also need practice to be able to get better and better so that you can eventually add back in at least a few of those questions we originally wanted you to skip. Practice is integral to our strategy.

That being said, even if you are taking the ACT tomorrow, you should still apply the basis of the strategy, if not the strategy itself. While we don't recommend that you skip a passage, we do suggest that you focus on quality over quantity, which will help you improve your score. For example, if you get to a question that you think you just need an extra 30 seconds to get right, spend those 30 seconds and try to get the answer correct. This isn't as risky as skipping a passage without practice, but it starts to prepare your mind to focus on quality, which is what you really need to do well on the ACT.

4. I'm not taking the ACT tomorrow, but I only have a week or two to prepare. What do I do?

Well, you definitely don't have time to practice enough to make the entire strategy effective. But, you may have enough time to implement part of the strategy effectively. What we recommend you do is pick one section of the ACT and focus on it. When students come to us, we tell them to pick the section that they like the most (or dislike the least).

Normally, students have no trouble picking a section they prefer. Every once in a while, though, we have a student who likes (or dislikes) all sections of the ACT equally. If that's you, we recommend starting with the Science section. Why the Science section? The English and Math sections both require outside knowledge, and one to two weeks is not enough time to acquire and become fully accustomed to using new knowledge. So, that leaves Reading or Science. With the Reading section, if the student isn't a "reader," one or two weeks is likely not long enough to do a sufficient amount of practice. With the Science, because almost no outside knowledge is required, all you need to do during those one or two weeks is become better at finding information in tables and graphs. That will still require a lot of hard work, but it's, generally, more easily accomplished.

No matter which section you pick, we recommend you begin by doing a few practice sections untimed. Ideally, we want you to do as many practice sections as you need to do until you start having the number of answers correct that we ask of our students according to our strategy. Once you get to that point, or once the ACT is a few days away, start doing timed sections. There will, hopefully, be enough time for you to do at least five practice sections, and that will be enough for you to see some score improvement on that section.

5. When I register for the ACT, does it matter where I choose to take it?

We think it does. If it's offered at your own school, try to take the test there every time. That way, you're comfortable with your surroundings and will experience just a little bit less anxiety (i.e., you have the home advantage). To do that, be sure to register early so you can make sure to reserve a spot there.

If you aren't able to take the test at your school, try to create a home advantage at another location. How? Pick a location where you think you'd be comfortable, and try to register for that location every time you take the test (unless, of course, that place turns out to be horrible for some reason, in which case, try a different place the second time). Familiarity is helpful when it comes to taking the ACT, so don't underestimate it.

6. How many times should I take the ACT?

We recommend you take the ACT three to five times. More specifically, we want you to take it at least that many times on TIR administrations. (For more information on the TIR, see Chapter 10.) Clearly, you don't have to register for a TIR administration if you are absolutely sure that it will be the last time you will be taking the test. However, we find that some of our students stick with a TIR administration anyway, because after spending so much time with us (hearing us talk about quality), they become acutely interested in how they did.

Other than maximizing performance, the number of times you take the ACT becomes important when you send your scores to colleges and universities. We recommend that you not send your scores to schools at all. None of them. Instead, when you know you're done taking the ACT for good, go online and send your best score report to the colleges and universities to which you are applying. However, there are a few institutions that might require you to disclose all of your ACT scores, so you should check with the schools to which you are applying.

Some colleges, universities, and scholarship foundations say they will "superscore." Superscoring is when an institution takes the best score in each section (English, Math, Reading, Science) from all of your ACT administrations and generates a new composite (average) from those four section scores.

We're always ambivalent when we have a student who asks about superscoring. With some schools that superscore, we agree that it's a good idea to send the tests showing all your best section scores. With some highly selective universities, however, even if they're willing to superscore, consider whether, in your particular situation, it's really a good idea to send them multiple score reports. For example, let's say you took the ACT four times and, on the English section, earned a 19, 27, 30, and 31. You might not want an admissions or scholarship committee to see the 19, even if the score report with the 19 somehow contains your highest Science score.

7. What is the best month to take the ACT?

Without question, the best month to take the ACT is June. We think so for two reasons. The first is that it is one of the TIR administrations, which means that you can order the TIR and carefully analyze your results. (For more information on the TIR, see Chapter 10.) That will allow you to better focus your practice time towards targeting your weaknesses, instead of just practicing everything.

The second reason is that the June administration usually provides you with the opportunity for added, uninterrupted practice time before the ACT. Why? Because it's the only ACT not offered during the school year. Some students only have a few days between the end of the school year and the June ACT; others have a whole a week or two. Either way, that translates into practice time that is free from the interference of school, which is a bonus that the other ACT administrations can't offer you.

However, if you plan on taking the June ACT, we recommend that you begin preparing at least as early as the spring months while you're in school and then really kick into high gear and practice a ton after school lets out.

8. What do I need to take with me to the ACT on test day?

First, consult the ACT website (www.actstudent.org) for the items that you must, can, and cannot bring with you to the test.

Other than that, we have a few suggestions. First, it is very important that you use the exact same calculator that you used during practice. And we mean the exact same one. We recommend that you use a graphing calculator, like the TI-84, and *not* a regular scientific calculator. There are a number of shortcuts you can do with the graphing calculator, which will be included in our ACT Math content book (coming soon).

Next, bring an analog watch, preferably one with a bezel (which you should learn to use), especially if time is an issue for you. Digital watches are risky, because if they have a timer and it happens to go off during the test, you may be disqualified. If you don't have an analog watch and plan on buying one, don't buy it the night before the test. Instead, get it now so that you can practice with it. (We've added a link on the *Resources* page of our website to an example of an inexpensive analog watch with a bezel).

Always bring a whole bunch of sharpened #2 pencils. You don't want to deal with sharpening pencils, broken pencils, or raising your hand and asking the proctor to lend you one of her measly, sub-par pencils. When we take the ACT, we take in around 10 sharpened #2 pencils.

Also, bring a snack. The best kind is something that will give you some quick energy via sugar (e.g., a granola bar with chocolate or raisins).

9. Do I get a break on test day?

Yes, the ACT provides you with a "short break" between the Math and Reading sections. Usually, it's about 10 to 15 minutes long.

It's important to use the break wisely. Go to the bathroom (whether you need to or not). Then, go walk around, preferably the entire time (the movement will get your energy up), and eat your snack.

During the break, remind yourself that at the end of the Math section, you aren't only halfway done (as most AJs think); you are probably more than two-thirds of the way done, if you're measuring by total amount time you'll be at the test center. In fact, at that point, the test will be over in a little more than an hour. So, pump yourself up during the break instead of letting yourself wear down. Doing so can be a big benefit because everyone else is feeling fatigued and ready to go home, which means that if you can keep your energy up, you're in a better position to outperform other test takers. Also, during the break, remind yourself that the last two sections are the trickiest and

142

that you'll need a heightened sense of awareness to avoid the ACT's pitfalls and to do well on those sections.

10. How do I build up my stamina for the ACT?

This is a great question. Fatigue and conditioning are two of the most underestimated factors affecting student performance on the ACT. The best way to deal with fatigue is to practice real ACT tests. Good practice starts with untimed tests but eventually moves on to timed sections and finally on to timed whole tests.

Remember, if possible, on at least the four Saturdays leading up to test day, force yourself to wake up early and take a full practice test at 8 a.m. That will help condition you to have the mental stamina for the actual test.

11. Can I skip more questions than you recommend?

In Chapter 4, we talked about two kinds of AJs: the AJs who rush through the test, finish it, but get a lot wrong, and the AJs who do very well on a relatively small portion of the test and end up guessing a lot on the rest of it. You don't want to be either kind of AJ. While there is certainly some flexibility in our strategy, as a general answer, we're inclined to say no. Don't skip more questions than we recommend.

However, there is some wiggle room in our strategy for how many questions you answer and how many you guess. It all depends on your target score. If you just want to improve your score on a particular section to, say, a 22, then you may not need to complete as many questions, but we recommend that you do your best to stick to the strategy anyway.

The way that you figure out the right balance between the quality and quantity needed to achieve your target score is by doing practice tests and scoring them (as we have shown you) using the raw score conversion table *for that specific test*. If you find, in your practicing, that you are getting the questions you do correct but taking so long that you only get half of the passages done, that tells you that you need to continue practicing until you become efficient enough that the balance between quality and quantity is more reasonable. Again, practice is key to making the strategy work.

12. What if I want a score higher than a 25?

We love that. We want our students to earn the highest possible score they can, and our strategy can absolutely help you do that.

You now know that our motto is "Quality over Quantity." Eliminating passages in order to give test takers more time is simply a practical application of that motto. It forces test takers to slow down and focus on quality rather than worrying about quantity. In essence, what the strategy teaches you to do is to become a good test taker (i.e., one of those students located in the 30% zone of the bell curve). If you recall, those students finish the test (or most of it) with very few errors. Their quality is impeccable, and our strategy teaches you to mimic that feature as you move towards becoming a better test taker. But, it all depends on how much you're willing to practice.

Why is that? With enough practice and familiarity with the test, a cool thing starts to happen. At first, just work on trying to adhere to the strategy. Once you get good at it and start taking timed practice sections, you'll notice that you may only have 30 seconds or so left when you've done all of the passages except the skip passage. Thirty seconds is just enough time to bubble in guesses for the remaining questions in the skip passage, but nothing else. After some practice, however, you'll get better at the ACT and naturally become a little faster, so you'll find yourself with maybe two minutes of time when you get to the skip passage. That means you can do a few of those questions before having to guess on the rest. After more practice, you'll find yourself with five minutes of time at the end, which translates into more questions correct in the skip passages and an even higher score. After even more practice, you may find yourself with enough time to complete the skip passage.

Where does this time come from? It comes from the fact that you become an expert on this test. You have done so much practice and so many questions that you become extremely familiar with the ACT, and answering its questions becomes routine. When you get faster at answering ACT questions, it takes less time to get through a section without having to sacrifice the accuracy you've already acquired by practicing our strategy.

13. I increased my score 5 points after my first cycle of practice! If I do another cycle, my score will rise another 5 points, right?

We wish we could say yes, but it really depends on the person.

Consider this question: is it easier to go from a score of 17 to a score of 22, from a score of 22 to a score of 27, or is it exactly the same? You might think it would be the same. After all, you're moving up five points each time.

Generally speaking, in order to go from a score of 17 to 22, what you need to learn is fundamentals, i.e., those things that frequently show up on the ACT. In order to go from a score of 22 to 27, you need to both retain the fundamentals that you learned when you increased your score from 17 to 22 and to learn how to tackle less commonly tested questions. There are more uncommon question *types* that occasionally appear on the ACT than the common ones typically mastered in the first practice cycle. So, more effort is required to take your score from a 22 to a 27!

Also, in order to do better on the ACT, you need to make fewer careless errors. You can make a lot of careless mistakes and still score a 17, and when you retake the test, if you make fewer careless mistakes, you might be able to increase your score to a 22. To raise your score still further to a 27, you have to make significantly fewer mistakes than you made when you got a 22, and that takes a lot of practice and focus. That doesn't mean it's not possible; it's just harder to do.

Lastly, keep in mind that everyone improves at a different pace. For some of our students, they progress very linearly and raise their scores by about the same amount each time they take the ACT. Some of our students have to take multiple ACTs before they see significant improvement; all of a sudden, things seem to click for them, and their scores shoot way up. Other students we've tutored improved their scores greatly after their first practice cycle, but then saw only marginal improvement in subsequent administrations. It takes different test takers

146

different amounts of time and practice before they master the various kinds of questions tested on the ACT.

Bottom line: if your score improves a significant amount the first time you implement our strategy on the ACT, don't take it as a guarantee that the exact amount of improvement will happen again in the next cycle. It could be more; it could be less. Either way, keep practicing until you reach your target score.

14. What letter should I choose when I guess?

This is probably the question we're asked the most. The answer is: it doesn't matter. It really honestly and truly does not matter. What does matter is that you're spending time thinking about something that isn't practical. Based on our experience, the likelihood of each letter being correct is pretty evenly distributed. But even if a university study revealed that answer choice **C** (or **H**), for example, is the most common answer ever, it doesn't mean that it will be the most common answer on your ACT or even on a particular section or in a specific passage on which you guess.

To be honest, we're not big fans of these types of questions, because they're based on a superstitious belief and are symptomatic of an AJ mentality. They're definitely not indicative of a focus on quality over quantity, which is how we'd prefer you think. So, stop thinking about it.

Another common example of a test-taking behavior based on a superstitious belief is the conviction that if you bubbled **A** (or **F**), for example, four times in a row, the next answer can't be **A**. Students actually alter their answers on a test based on this belief. But even if you could be assured (and you can't, because we've seen it be right) that the same answer will not repeat a certain number of times in a row, how do you know which one of your answers is wrong? Why assume the last one is the one that's wrong (as most students do)? You, hopefully, had a good reason for choosing each of them so you should trust your previous decisions. That's why we think you should abandon superstitions like these, and rely, instead, on a logical, math-based, proven approach.

The ACT spends exactly zero time worrying about what arrangement of answers they have on a test, and that's how much time you should spend worrying about it too. We have never seen any indication that one letter is used more than the others as a correct answer, and we certainly have seen times when multiple correct answers with the same letter (or location) appear back-to-back. So what should you guess for all those questions in passages we taught you to skip? Just pick any letter now, stick with it, and let the superstitions go.

15. Should I get a tutor?

Of course, we're biased. So, we think that if you have the resources to hire a tutor, it is a good idea. An experienced ACT tutor with a proven track record who can show you how to work those Math or English problems that you just can't puzzle through is a great thing to have. Setting up a regular time with a tutor is also a good way to make sure you are staying disciplined and spending a good amount of time practicing.

With that in mind, we want to remind you that, in the same way that there are bad teachers and bad professors, there are bad tutors. Try to hire a tutor that your friends (or even your friends' older siblings) have found helpful. A bad or unhelpful tutor is, clearly, not worth the time or money.

In short, if you can, hire a good tutor. If not, find the discipline to study by yourself and identify a couple of good teachers willing to help you with questions that stump you.

16. What are the differences between the ACT and the SAT?

On the surface, they seem similar. The ACT's English section is comparable to the SAT's Writing section (not to be confused with the essay portion of the SAT). Both the ACT and SAT have a Math section. The ACT's Reading section seems comparable to the SAT's Critical Reading section. The ACT has an optional essay, and the SAT has a required essay. So, superficially, the one major difference is that the ACT has a Science section and the SAT does not.

Geographically, some states are ACT-dominant and some states are SAT-dominant. The reasons are mostly historical; it has nothing to do with the tests themselves. In general, the states along and closer to the East and West coasts of the U.S. tend to be more SAT-dominant, while those in the middle of the U.S. tend to be more ACT-dominant. Almost every university and college in the U.S. will accept either test and has no preference.

The ACT was developed primarily as an achievement test, or a test that measures knowledge. That's true for the English and the Math sections, but our experience tells us that it isn't really an achievement test for the Reading or Science sections. In fact, a 2011 study by the National Bureau of Economic Research found that the English and Math sections (but not the Reading or Science sections) of the ACT are good predictors of success in college. (If you're interested, a link to the report is available on our website under *Resources.*) The SAT, on the other hand, was originally based on an IQ test, and it still has remnants of those kinds of questions.

17. Should I take the ACT or the SAT?

You can prepare and do well on both tests. The SAT tends to be a much more tricky test throughout, whereas a larger proportion of the ACT questions tend to be straightforward. The ACT, in general, really only tends to be tricky on the Reading and Science sections (which isn't surprising because those sections aren't emphasizing outside knowledge). The SAT Math section tends to ask fewer questions that are common in school than the ACT Math section (whose questions often look a lot like your math homework). The SAT also relies heavily on vocabulary, the kind with which most high school students are unfamiliar.

We not only think the SAT will be tougher for most students, but also that it will be a tougher test for most students to improve their scores on. However, that doesn't mean you can't take the SAT and do well. We have students every year that work hard and do very well on the SAT. Every test can be prepared for and mastered.

Some people say that if you're not good at science, you shouldn't take the ACT because it has a science section, unlike the SAT. But if you read Chapter 8, you know that's not a good reason not to take the ACT because the Science section requires no real outside knowledge of science.

We've heard some people say that you should take both and see which one you perform better on, but we disagree. Most students are not innately good at either of these tests. Even if you take both, how do you know that you didn't have an "off day" while taking one and an "on day" while taking the other? And even if that's not the case, if you do better on one and worse on the other, how do you know you won't improve faster through practice on the one you did worse on?

So which one do we recommend you take? It doesn't matter! Just pick one. If you're not sure, just pick the ACT because it is the test where outside knowledge and strategy can be more easily applied. But it really doesn't matter. The worst mistake you can make is to work on both of them at the same time, because everyone only has a finite amount of time to prepare. Splitting time between the two tests risks your becoming mediocre at both instead of becoming really good at one of them.

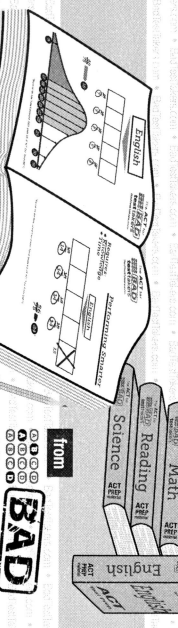